BIOGRAPHIES
OF OUR *Maternal*
FAMILY HISTORY

Thompson Family History Biographies

Vol. 9, Ed. 1

We're all ghosts.

We all carry, inside us, people who came before us

- Liam Callanan

Including Mazo/Mason, Brown (2), Thompson (2), Shatteen, Morgan, Forsythe, Hampton, Washington, Robinson, Curry, Glover, Frazier et al of Nassau, Bahamas; Africa; Chatham, Jefferson & Washington Counties, GA; and Allendale, Barnwell & Beaufort Counties, SC; Romano, DiSimone, Vitale, Viviano, Carmona, Quintavalle, McCabe, Smith, O'Connor/Connor, Morrison of Sicilia, Italy and Ireland to New York, NY and reference to Barrett, Kilmartin/Gilmartin, Reilly (2), McLean, Brown, Boles, Nocton, DiStefano, Cutumachio, Tully, Kirrane, McGowan et al of Counties Cavan, Mayo & Sligo, Ireland; Palermo, Italy; New York, NY and PA: Wittle, Hummer, Kyle, Whitmoyer, Minick, Yaeger, Sheets, McKim, Stewart, Smith, McKinsey, Fry, Shover, Piper, Shannon, Swoveland, Acri (2), Curcio, Barbuscio Marsico, Buglio, Magnelli, DeStephano, Martino, Sammarco, et al of Ireland; Calabria, Sicily, Italy; Baden-Wurttemberg, Lower Saxony & Rhineland-Palatinate, Germany; and Cumberland, Dauphin, Franklin, Lancaster, Perry & York Counties, PA.

Marc D. Thompson

Jack Butler

Front Cover Photo: Shirley Duncan (right), Melvalean Curry
Thompson (left) & Sophia Thompson (center)

Published by:

VirtuFit Delray Beach, FL
www.marcdthompson.net
info@marcdthompson.net

ISBN: 978-1945376993

© 2017 Marc D. Thompson

OTHER BOOKS BY AUTHOR

DEDICATION

This volume is dedicated to all our family and friends, who selflessly donated information, time, effort, research and love to make this compilation possible.

ACKNOWLEDGEMENTS

Thanks to my parents, my sisters, and my children for the knowledge and support. Thanks to my history teachers through high school and college and to Ray from Pennsylvania State Library for his early tutelage.

Thanks to my hundreds of cousins, near and far, who have donated their time as well as their long-toiled family histories and to every clerk, registrar, cemetery manager, LDS employee, ancestry.com staff and others who researched in places I couldn't visit. Thanks the amazing literary talents of Jack Butler and Gary Rosenberg. This book is truly the love of thousands.

CONTENTS

FOREWORD

by Shirley M. Duncan

Why do people seek to learn about their family history? Years ago, Marc asked me for information about our relatives. He was eager to start the journey into the past. As of today, I believe Marc has answered the question. He wanted to view our lives more fully.

Marc enjoys solving the multitude of mysteries regarding family histories and it is revealed in his family history volumes. While visiting Marc, he asked me to visit a local library to search for information regarding a family's ancestor. Fortunately, I found the information Marc needed.

Suddenly, I realized how searching for long ago addresses, pictures, and families is a wonderful way to reflect back to how and why things happened; in a way, making sense of it all! Marc truly knows how to present the past to each of us as we look toward the future. Allow his thirty years of research skill and efforts take you on a journey around the world!

PROLOGUE

by Marc D. Thompson

If I were given the opportunity to live in any era, I would most certainly pick the 1870s. The time was simple and the people were honest. Folks worked hard and took pride in their families, their homes and their reputations. When I look into the eyes of our ancestors from that time period, I feel a link; I would have fit nicely in their time.

Some housekeeping points:

- In most cases, the Anglicized first and middle names were used; e.g., Johann Heinrich is John Henry and Orsala Francesca is Ursula Frances.

- The most commonly found surname was used, whether Anglicized or not.

- The female maiden name was used in most cases, except occasionally when with husband; e.g., photograph of family or double burial headstones.

- The majority of the collateral information was derived from the U.S. Census records and data from cousins' compilations.

- Place names were documented as precisely as possible, using the name of the place as it was at that time in history. For example, parts of Germany were once Prussia, parts of Lebanon

County, Pennsylvania were once Lancaster County, Pennsylvania, etc.

- In some cases, the common name was used. Before Pennsylvania's statehood, although it was the Swedish Colony and later the Province of Pennsylvania, simply Pennsylvania was used. Lastly, to preserve privacy, all information on living persons has been removed or privatized.

- In the photo section, these abbreviations are used. r-right, l-left, c-center, w.-with, MNU-maiden name unknown, arrow-pictured under arrow

- I-signifies first ancestors of similar name and II, III designates later generation ancestor with same name, not necessarily father and son

Who we are cannot be separated from where we're from.
- Malcolm Gladwell

INTRODUCTION

Genealogy is a lifelong duty. The day we were born or the day we bore children ourselves, we earned a responsibility of passing along our history. We are responsible for the knowledge of our parents and of our grandparents and all their wisdom.

Our duty, therefore, is our heritage—including the names and faces of our forefathers and mothers, the medical history and genetic backgrounds of their blood lines, the princes and the paupers, the photographs and historical places, the tragedies and the joys.

The ancient Scottish bards memorized their royal families, reciting the pedigrees of the Old Scot's Kings regardless of the complexity. The Irish kings would pass down their regal history orally. They would recite a list of names—their kin—noting outstanding events associated with the forbearers. West African families passed down stories from generation to generation.

On and on, the mnemonic Peruvians, the beads of New Zealand, the Indian Cera Kings, the extensive Chinese genealogies, the ancient Japanese string of names. Argument could be said that ALL family have the need for knowledge of their genealogy.

Genealogy was created in order for people to know the history of their lineage, to discover their origins, and to prove blood-lines and royalty. This volume was compiled in response to our deep desire to understand and discover their past. It shall stand as part of the legacy of our ancestry. Our ancestors had wisdom and understanding. They had goals, glories, and personalities.

Our forty-year journey has led to the numerous genealogy volumes and updates of previous volumes. Many genealogies tend to trace a descendant line or the paternal line (single ascendancy). Our purpose was to trace all ancestors with equal perseverance back in time. This is a monumental—if not near impossible—task. We have compiled a pedigree, beginning with our children and with the current emphasis on generations one through ten, although we have completed research as far back as generation 21. Additional collateral ancestral data have begun to be added as of 2015.

The mission of our genealogy books is four fold. First, to amass photographs—as a face can tell a thousand tales—as so much can be learned from them. The second goal is to document the medical background of our ancestors, so our children can lead a healthier life. The third goal is to continue to extend the lineage in order to link to as many relatives as possible. Our final goal leads us to the building of narratives from this amassed information, producing a readable experience of our ancestors and their lives.

Our ancestors are not mere names or dates—they have tales to tell, journeys to document, lives to discover. They have accomplishments and setbacks, which in turn help us with ours. As we mentioned "Who we are cannot be separated from where we're from," this book therefore allows us to know precisely where we're from.

CHAPTER ONE: WHAT'S IN A NAME

Fame is the inheritance not of the dead, but of the living.
It is we who look back with lofty pride to
the great names of antiquity.
- William Hazlitt

Our children, as with all life, represent the beginning of all things. They are bore and they begin their life-long experiences. Here they are the beginning of our book, back from which we narrate to bring their ancestors to life. Our children, nephews and nieces were all born from 1980–2010. Here are some of the meanings behind our children's names.

Our children's Names and Derivation

I guess it's hard not to agree,
You say it all depends of money
And who's in your family tree.
-   Supertramp

Adam: This is the Hebrew word for "man." It could be ultimately derived from Hebrew Adam meaning "to be red," referring to the ruddy color of human skin, or from Akkadian adamu meaning "to make." According to Genesis in the Old Testament Adam was created from the earth by God. There is a word play on Hebrew adamah meaning "earth." He and Eve were supposedly the first humans, living happily in the Garden of Eden until Adam ate a forbidden fruit given to him by Eve. As an English Christian name, Adam has been common since the Middle Ages, and it received a boost after the Protestant Reformation. A famous bearer was Scottish economist Adam Smith.

Andrew: English form of the Greek name Andreas, which was derived from andreios "manly, masculine," a derivative of aner "man." In the New Testament the apostle Andrew, the first disciple to join Jesus, is the brother of Simon Peter. According to tradition, he later preached in the Black Sea region, with some legends saying he was crucified on an X-shaped cross. Andrew, being a Greek name, was probably only a nickname or a translation of his real Hebrew name, which is not known. This name has been common throughout the Christian world, and it became very popular in the Middle Ages. Saint Andrew is regarded as the patron of Scotland, Russia, Greece and Romania. The name has been borne by three kings of Hungary, American president Andrew Jackson and, more recently, English composer Andrew Lloyd Webber.

Ashley: From an English surname which was originally derived from place names meaning "ash tree clearing," from Old English Aesc and Leah. Until the 1960s it was more commonly given to boys in the United States, but it is now most often used on girls.

Connor: Anglicized form of the Gaelic name Conchobhar which means "dog lover" or "wolf lover." It has been in use in Ireland for centuries and was the name of several Irish kings. It was also borne by the legendary Ulster King Conchobar mac Nessa, known for his tragic desire for Deirdre.

Marie: French and Czech form of Maria. A notable bearer of this name was Marie Antoinette, a queen of France, and Marie Curie, a physicist and chemist who studied radioactivity with her husband Pierre. Latin form of Greek from Hebrew Mary. Maria is the usual form of the name in many European languages, as well as a secondary form in other languages such as English. In some countries, for example Germany, Poland and Italy, Maria is occasionally used as a masculine middle name. This was the name of two ruling queens of Portugal. It was also borne by the Habsburg queen Maria Theresa, whose inheritance of the domains of her father, the Holy Roman Emperor Charles VI, began the War of the Austrian Succession. The meaning is not known for certain, but there are several theories including "sea of bitterness," "rebelliousness," and "wished for child." However, it was most likely originally an Egyptian name, perhaps derived in part from my "beloved" or my "love."

Renae: French form of Renatus. A famous bearer was the French mathematician and rationalist philosopher René Descartes. Late Latin name meaning "born again."

Roman: From the Late Latin name Romanus which meant "Roman."

Sophia: Means "wisdom" in Greek. This was the name of an early, probably mythical, saint who died of grief after her three daughters were martyred. Legends about her probably arose as a result of a medieval misunderstanding of the phrase Hagia.

Sophia: "Holy Wisdom," which was the name of a large basilica in Constantinople. This name was common among continental European royalty during the Middle Ages, and it was popularized in Britain by the German House of Hanover when they inherited the British throne in the 18th century. It was the name of characters in the novels Tom Jones by Henry Fielding and The Vicar of Wakefield by Oliver Goldsmith.

Our Ancestor's Contributions and Facts

Through the research of the TFH, we have discovered that we are related to some famous and infamous folks, and even found that there are some areas of the world named for our distant families.

We are direct-line descendants of William Duke of Jülich-Cleves-Berg and Maria of Austria, Duchess of Jülich-Cleves-Berg, Countess Clothilde de Valois de Reni and Jacques de Sellaire, Von Zeller of Castle Zellerstein of Zurich, John Thomson of Haddington, Johann La Hentzelle of Lorraine, General John Benfield of Normandy, Henri Banage de Beauval of Rouen, Alexander Thompson of Schuylkill, the Guerne family of Eschert, the Bager family of Wiesbaden, the Emmerich family of Delkenheim, the Batdorf family of Darmstadt, the Gaukel family of Miltenberg and the Lotz family of the Palatinate.

We are direct-line descendants of soldiers who sacrificed for our freedom: Civil War servicemen Andrew G. Hensel and Daniel Updegrove, and possibly Elijah Anderson and Thomas E. Batdorf. War of 1812 servicemen Adam Frantz, Andrew W. Hensel and Joseph Workman, and possible William Row and John Gipe. Revolutionary War servicemen Andrew Messerschmidt, Andrew Miller, Frank Row, Henry Bucher, Jacob Lehman, Jacob Livezey, Jacob Philip Bordner, Jacob Rudy, John Adam Guise, John Balthaser Romberger, John

Casper Hensel, John Conrad Bucher, John Daniel Angst, John Faber, John George Herrold, John George Schupp, John Henry Reiman, John Jacob Loyman John Miller, John Peter Braun (British), John Peter Shaffer, Jonas Rudy, Michael Garman, Michael Leyman, Nicholas Mantz, Peter Keefer, Valentine Welker, and William Anderson.

Our children's maternal lines include WWII servicemen Ed Mazo, Percy Forsythe and Robert Forsythe; WWI serviceman Raymond Barbush; and Civil War servicemen Cyrus Shannon, Jacob Wittle, John Shover, John Minnick, and Sebastian Shover. We are collateral descendants of Presidents Dwight D. Eisenhower and William McKinley; Pennsylvania politicians Samuel Pennypacker, John Morton, and Jonas Row; Civil War Brigadier General Galushia Penny- packer; entertainers Marlon Brando, Les Brown, and Ray W. Brown; religious leaders Conrad Weiser and Michael Enderline; and famed Melba Dodge, Jesse Runkle, Enrico Caruso, and Galla Curci. Lastly, Taylor Wittel lists relations to James Madison, Zachary Taylor, Jefferson Davis, and Gene Autry.

Our ancestors' names have been immortalized at these locations: the Bager Homestead, Abbottstown, Pennsylvania; the Chris Miller Homestead, North Lebanon Township, Pennsylvania; the Benfield homestead, Berks Co., Pennsylvania; the Livesey Homestead, Philadelphia, Pennsylvania; the Wirth Homestead, Dauphin Co., Pennsylvania; the Keefer Homestead in Berks,

Pennsylvania; the Morton Homestead in Chester, Pennsylvania; the Herrold Homestead in Northumberland, Pennsylvania; and the Jacob Lehman Homestead in Hanover, Pennsylvania. Additionally, these place names were named after our forbearers: Bordnersville, Kelly Crossroads, Livesey Street, Herrold's Island, Keefer's Station, Deibler's Gap, Deibler's Dam, and Shoemakertown, all in Pennsylvania.

The approximate percentages of relative's birthplaces are: 45% born in Pennsylvania, 17% Germany, 14% Scotland, 9% Italy, 4% Georgia, 4% South Carolina, 4% Ireland, 2% New York, and 1% Africa, Virginia, Florida, Switzerland, England, Bohemia, France, Sweden, Finland, and the West Indies.

At the moment, our paternal line breaks down to about 11/16 German, 3/16 Britain, 1/16 French, 1/16 Swiss. Our maternal line breaks down to about 10/16 German, 4/16 Britain, 1/16 French, 1/16 Swiss/Scandinavian. Our children's maternal lines break down to 7/16 Italian, 4/16 African, 2/16 Irish, 2/16 German, 1/16 West Indian/Britain.

By the Numbers

3 Ancestors who died at sea: N. Benesch, G. Reith & G. Shoemaker
3 Ancestors named Ashley or Renae
5 Number of birth states
8 Ancestors named Gerald or Gilbert
8 Most different lines with same surname: Miller, Mueller, etc.
10 Generations, FTM lines only (numerous)
11 Number of birth countries
14 Youngest age having child, female: Anna Maria Hamm & Anna Barbara Knerr
17 Youngest age having child, male, John George Werner
17 Number of children, one couple, Mary Louisa Peters/ Thomas Edward Batdorf
18 Youngest age at death, female: Emma Keefer
21 Generations, FTM & additional lines (Livesay)
22 Number of children, one man, Isabelle Penman & Mary Bast/Alexander Thompson
24 Ancestors named Sophia or Marie
24 Most letters in name, male: Howard Andrew Carson Hensel
27 Most letters in name, female: Amelia Dorothy Elizabeth Bager
30 Youngest age at death, male: William Duncan
34 Ancestors named Andrew or Roman 34 Media records, collateral lines
50 Oldest age having child, female: Veronica Schmidt
50 Most variations for single surname: Batdorf, Bodorff, Batterff, Pottorf, etc.
57 Ancestors named Connor or Adam
59.6 Average lifespan, all lines
63.2 Average lifespan, Thompson lines
68 Oldest age having child, male: Alexander Thompson
94 Oldest age at death: Sarah Faber, Anna Bleymeyer & Michael Goodman
256 Ancestors named Shirley or Mary
412 Media records, Thompson lines
491 Media records, all lines
569 Direct-line ancestors, Thompson lines
776 Place names, Thompson lines
870 Direct-line ancestors, all lines
923 Sources used, Thompson lines
983 Total surnames, Thompson line
1,328 Sources used, all lines
1,371 Place names, all lines
1,230 Total surnames, all lines
4,675 Sources checked, Thompson lines
5,801 Relatives, Thompson lines
5,825 Sources checked, all lines
8,569 Relatives, all lines
1410 Earliest birth, unrecorded lines, Geoffrey Livesay
1689 Earliest birth, recorded lines, John Wendel George Traut

This and the proceeding Family History narratives are our heritage. With this information we can be proud of ourselves and our past, and aim toward bright futures and better lives. If our duty is neglected, as each generation passes, so will our family history.

We have a desire and we have a bond. We have a desire to know from whence we came. We want to know our history, our origins. We want to know what our ancestors did, how they persevered and how the spark of life made its way from Geoffrey Livesay, born over 600 years ago, to our latest cousin, born just this winter 2015.

CHAPTER TWO: CURRY FAMILY

The history of the American Negro
is the history of this strife,
He simply wishes to make it possible for a man
to be both a Negro and an American...
- W.E.B. Du Bois

Our Curry and Mazo (originally Mason) families were located in the deep South, part of Georgia and South Carolina. We are indebted to their struggles and pain, and the ultimate triumph to bring us freedom and opportunity.

Generation Two

Our parents are including in the second generation, comprising those born in from about 1910 to 1950. Those living are not included in this book, so this is the only narrative for this family included in this book.

A family is like a forest, when you are outside it is dense, when you are inside you see that each tree has its place.

-- African Proverb

Eddie Mazo & Dolores A. Curry

The baby boy who would become Eddie Mazo was born to Mack Mason and Sarah Thompson of Jefferson County, Georgia, on September 7, 1912. Edward was born their fifth child, joining a family that already included two older brothers and two older sisters, Jesse, John, Annie Lee, and Maria. After Edward's birth, siblings Mack, Robert, and Melvin were born to the Masons.

Mack and Sarah Mason named their son Edward Mason after Mack's father, Edward "Ned" Mason. The senior Edward held a special position in the family based on the fact that he represented the last generation of this Mason family to be born a slave. He had had been freed as a young man by Abraham Lincoln's Emancipation Proclamation and guaranteed equality of rights by the 13th, 14th, and 15th Amendments to the U.S. Constitution.

Unfortunately, as soon as Georgia was readmitted to the Union in 1871—the last previously Confederate state to be accepted— Federal troops started pulling out. With the direct threat reduced, former Confederates and their offspring began trying every political trick they could to keep the black Georgians from achieving equality with the whites. By 1916, every black person in Georgia had come to understand the wide gap between what the Federal Government promised and what the state and local governments delivered. Just before Edward Mason's birth, the State of Georgia had gone so far as to issue an official State charter for the rebirth of the Ku Klux Klan, which had been closed down and wiped out by the Federal troops.

To be sure, black people were organizing and working for change—more than a million and a half left the south and moved to the industrial cities of the Northeast and Midwest. The NAACP had been formed in New York in 1909, and was heavily pushing court cases to end lynchings and overturn the Jim Crow laws that legalized racial segregation. They were having some successes, but progress was slow and the families that stayed in Georgia still had lives to live as best they could.

Mack Mason worked hard to provide for his family, sometimes as a farm laborer or a stable hand, and sometimes as a sharecropper farmer. But even for a hard-working man, jobs were not always available for a laborer in rural Georgia. Mack and his family often had to follow opportunity from place to place. When Edward Mason was born, Mack was working as a day laborer at a saw mill in Louisville, Georgia. Day laborers only work when there is a need for them—there was no assurance of working every day.

Circumstances following Edward's birth suggest that Sarah may have had a hard time with the birth, or may have suffered an illness afterwards. As already mentioned Edward was his mother's fifth child in nine years. The strain of so many children, combined with having to shift house and worry about money, may have been too heavy a load. Whatever the reason, the family apparently needed some relief—and the solution that they found would change Edward's life forever. They decided to send Edward to live with his Aunt Ida in her home in Atlanta, Georgia.

When Edward Mason came to her, Ida Jones, a recent widow, was a clothing presser for a department store. She was also already acting as a temporary surrogate mother for a niece named Jeraline Banks. Ida shared a house with three other adult women. Two of them worked outside the house, but one lady stayed at home and made her money by taking in laundry. Also, Jeraline was eleven years old when Edward came so she could act as playmate and sometimes as babysitter for him. She could always call the older woman for help if she needed it. This allowed Ida to work without worrying too much about having an adult close at hand if needed.

The arrangement between Mack and Sarah Mason and Aunt Ida was probably intended to be a temporary one—just a break meant to give Edward's folks a little rest and some breathing room. But month ran into month, and then year ran into year, and it turned out that Edward Mason lived with his Aunt Ida until he was fifteen years old. By then, Ida was referring to him as her son. During these years with Aunt Ida, Edward got most of his schooling, made friends, and first started noticing girls. It was also during these years with Ida that

Edward met a man named Mazo, a war hero, who family stories say made a great impression on young Edward and whom he came to greatly admire. Motivated by this admiration—and maybe also by some resentment towards a family that he felt had abandoned him—Edward took it on himself to change his name to Eddie Mazo.

By 1930, the times in Georgia and America had changed—and not for the better. The Jim Crow problems and the Great Depression had roared in, making life much tougher than it had been. Bread lines popped up around Atlanta, and men who had worked all their lives found themselves hoping for a handout. Like tens of thousands of other people, Aunt Ida—who was also getting older—lost her job with the department store. Her younger brother, Wallis Oliver, a recent widower, came to live with them. He, at least, was still working—also as a clothing presser. But even for people who still had jobs, wages were low, money was scarce, and living was difficult.

In April of that year, perhaps to alleviate some of the hardship on Ida, Eddie left his Aunt's house and went to live with the family of Jeraline Banks in Birmingham, Alabama. Henry Banks, Jeraline's father, and Gary Smith, Jeraline's new husband, still had jobs with a freight company. They loaded and unloaded trucks and worked in the warehouse.

The Banks family took Eddie in and called him their adopted son. Since Eddie worked in similar industries for much of his later life, it is likely they also got Eddie at least part-time work with them at some point. But one thing did not change. When the census taker came to the house that year, Eddie was listed as Edward Mazo. And that is how he always introduced himself.

Even though he never lived with his parents, it is likely that Eddie had at least occasional contact with some of his family. When he was in his early twenties, he moved to Savannah, Georgia, where most of the Masons were living at the time. He found a job there working with trucks for the State of Georgia. A few years later, he changed his job direction and found work as a cook.

In Savannah, Edward met and married a woman named Florence, and they soon had a daughter named Constance. The marriage very quickly appeared to be in trouble and continued up and down for some years. In November of 1945, with World War II all but over, the U.S. Army was still recruiting men for the huge job of bringing the boys home and returning U.S. installations to peacetime mode. Eddie enlisted in the Army Air Corps and spent nearly two years in Hawaii. It seems likely that at least part of his motivation was the chance to get away from his troubled marriage.

After he came home from the military, Eddie reunited briefly with Florence, but by the mid-fifties, the marriage was over. Eddie also had a daughter named Sarah with another woman, and he continued to live in Savannah, Georgia, for most of the remainder of his life. It is here in Savannah where Eddie would meet Delores Ann Curry.

Delores was born on February 24, 1948, in Savannah, Georgia, the child of Robert Joseph Forsyth and Cressie Jo Curry. Both of Delores's parents were also natives of Savannah, and Delores grew up and went to school there.

When Delores was in her late teens, she met Eddie and they had a daughter, Melvalean Curry, and a son, both born in the 1960s. Eddie was often not home and Delores had to raise the children with bare necessities. Opportunities for a single black woman with a family in the South were nearly nonexistent. Racism was still rampant and economic viability was low. Delores left Eddie shortly thereafter, moving to Philadelphia, Pennsylvania, and remarrying. She lived out her life in Philadelphia, and died there on December 16, 2000, at the age of 52.

In his last few years, Eddie had moved to Plains, Georgia, where he died on December 20, 1997. Eddie's World War II service in the Army Air Corps earned him the right of burial in a National Cemetery, and he was buried with honors in Section I, Row 682, of the Andersonville National Historic Site in Macon County, Georgia. This famous cemetery began during the Civil War as the final resting place for Union soldiers who perished while POWs at the nearby Confederate Camp Sumter, better known as Andersonville Prison

Camp. Eddie and Delores's daughter, Melvalean Curry Thompson, is the family's direct ancestor.

Generation Three

The four grandparents Sarah and Mack Mason and Cressie Jo and Robert J Forsyth comprise the Third Generation and is the starting point for the detailed biographies included in this volume. Their birth dates ranges from late 1800s to the early 1900s.

To place them in understandable location and time, the following information was downloaded from our ancestry.com FTM file. This brief biographical information, and the historical text that follows, will allow the reader to not only identify the starting point of the following biographies, but also allow a better understanding of the times, places and events.

I guess it hard not to agree,
You say it all depends on money,
And who's in your family tree.
\- Supertramp

The Ford Model T of 1908 was the first automobile mass produced on assembly lines with completely interchangeable parts. It was the automobile that opened up travel to the common middle-class. The innovation of the assembly line was revolutionary.

World War I, beginning in 1914, was a conflict involving most of the world's powers. The beginning of the war was sparked by the assassination of Archduke Franz Ferdinand of Austria Hungary. The world quickly formed into alliances, The Allied Powers—United Kingdom, France, The Russian Empire, and later the United States—fought against the Central Powers—The German Empire, The Austro-Hungarian Empire, The Ottoman Empire and the Kingdom of Bulgaria. Over 70 million military personnel fought in the war including 60 million Europeans. The Western Front consisted of a trench line that changed little until 1917. More than 15 million people were killed; making World War I one of the deadliest conflicts in history.

The Great Depression was a worldwide economic downturn that started with the stock market crash of 1929. The depression varied in countries around the world but generally started in 1929 and lasted until the beginning of World War II. Unemployment rose to 25% in the US and as high as 33% in other countries. Countries whose jobs primarily came from industry suffered the most. The Great Depression was the largest economic downturn in history.

The Holocaust refers to the systematic genocide of over six million European Jews by Nazi Germany. The genocide began in stages in the early 1930's by removing Jews from society; moving the Jews to concentration camps, where they died of slave labor and disease; moving Jews to ghettos; mass shootings in conquered territories; and finally extermination camps where most Jews who survived the journey were killed in gas chambers.

World War II began on September 1, 1939 with the German invasion of Poland. The war involved most of the world's powers and was divided into two sides: the Allies versus the Axis. World War II changed the boundaries of war with significant actions against civilians including the Holocaust and the only use of nuclear weapons in war. 100 million military personnel were involved in the conflict. World War II was the deadliest war in history with over 70 million casualties. World War II ended in 1945 with the victory of The Allies.

Mack Mason & Sarah A Thompson

The morning of September 25, 1880, came into Washington County, Georgia, cool and clear, with wide blue skies and light breezes. "Shirt-sleeve weather," the locals called it. It was so like all the other late September days in that part of Georgia it was only made memorable for Edward "Ned" Mason and his wife, Ranie, by the arrival of their newest son, Mack Mason.

Ned and Ranie had married young, and children had followed quickly and regularly, so that even though Ned and Ranie were only 33 and 27, respectively, Mack was their seventh child and their fifth son. Waiting to meet the new baby boy were older brothers George, Jim, Plum, and Austin, and sisters Jane and Dicey. And Mack would not be Ned and Ranie's last child—he would himself become older brother to two brothers, Alonzo and Oliver, and two sisters, Janice and Ella. Ned Mason and Ranie Brown had been born as slaves on the plantations of Washington County, Georgia. They had been freed by the Civil War and the Emancipation Proclamation. Mack and his brothers and sisters were the first generation to be born free.

As a slave, Mack Mason's father had been a farmhand and he continued to do that work for wages as a free man. But times were hard and pay was poor—everyone had to do what they could to help the family. This meant that education often took a backseat to financial need, and Mack only got through the fifth grade before he went to help, as had each of his brothers in their turn.

Mack Mason was born into a strange time in the lives of Georgia's freed slaves. For almost twenty years, African Americans in Georgia had been enjoying relatively mild political and racial relations with their white neighbors—which is what they had hoped for when emancipation had come.

To be sure, this favorable climate did not spring from good will on the part of former slave owners and Confederates who had started the Civil War in an effort to keep their slaves. Indeed, as soon as possible after the close of the Civil War, the former slave owners and Confederate veterans had regained control of the Georgia Legislature. They had then immediately passed harsh laws intended to remove the black man's recently granted right to vote and to physically and socially segregate black and white Georgians.

The U.S. Congress, though, totally controlled by Union men and in no mood to tolerate bad acts by former Confederates, brought out the hobnailed boots and kicked the white supremacists' plans to pieces. A series of new Federal laws intended to suppress the white supremacists' actions forced the former Confederates to backpedal. As a result, nearly all of the recently passed racist laws in the eleven former Confederate states were repealed by 1868. In addition, the 13th, 14th, and 15th Amendments to the U.S. Constitution were ratified with the intent of guaranteeing the former slaves and their descendants all of the rights due the white majority.

The effect of the Congressional actions was strong and immediate. Between 1867 and 1872, sixty-nine African Americans served as delegates to the Georgia State Constitutional Convention or as members of the Georgia State Legislature. Jefferson Franklin Long, a tailor from Bibb County, sat in the U.S. Congress from December 1870 to March 1871. Former slaves and slave owners shopped in the same stores, used the same banks, and walked on the same sidewalks.

With all of this forced change, Georgia was still a potentially dangerous place for the African American. A wrong word or even a particular glance at the wrong place or time could easily get a black man killed. Between 1880 and 1930, more than 450 men were lynched in Georgia, and prosecutions for those killings were rare.

But the years of Mack Mason's early childhood were times when, if they were a little careful, former slaves and their children could begin to feel, if not the full winds, surely the breezes of freedom. Mack, as a young boy going out to work, had little reason to suspect that, by his sixteenth birthday, events would create a very strong turn for the worse.

Having the Federal Government slap them down did not alter the segregationists' goal one iota. They still tested the waters on a regular basis by passing segregationist laws where they thought they might get away with it. In early 1872, Georgia schools were segregated. Then some cities and towns began mandating separate black and white cemeteries. But the real troubles began in 1883, when the U.S. Supreme Court ruled that, while the Federal Government could govern discrimination by other governmental bodies, the Constitution gave it no power over discrimination by individual citizens.

Former slave states saw this as a signal to start trying to expand the envelope on segregation. New restrictive laws were passed in the different states and some survived. Then in 1890, Louisiana passed a law requiring that railroads provide separate cars for blacks and whites. Determined to fight the law, a concerned group of prominent black, Creole, and white residents of New Orleans formed a Committee of Citizens with the stated purpose of attempting to repeal the law. The best thing, they decided, would be to create a case that would test the law in the courts. In 1892, one of the group—a mixed race man named Homer Plessy—bought a first-class ticket, boarded a "whites only" car, and found himself a seat. Mr. Plessy was immediately asked to move to the "blacks only" car, which he refused to do. He was arrested on the spot and the Committee of Citizens had their case.

The case, which was known as *Plessy vs Ferguson,* spent the next four years winding its way through the local and state courts.

Finally, in 1896, it came before the United States Supreme Court. As the Court convened for oral arguments on April 13, 1896, there was little to suggest that the ultimate outcome of *Plessy vs Ferguson* was going to be far worse for African Americans than anyone could have imagined.

Simply stated, the majority of the Supreme Court ruled that there was nothing in the Constitution, including the new 13th, 14th, and 15th Amendments, that prohibited the forced separation of the black and white races in public facilities. The Constitution, according to the Court, required that all citizens be protected equally, but that as long as the separate facilities provided to African Americans were equal to those provided to whites, no inherent violation of the U.S. Constitution would occur.

As each of the governments of the former slave states immediately perceived, the *Plessy* decision essentially legitimized the state laws establishing racial segregation in the South. All the various states had to do to totally exclude their black citizens from public places was to claim that separate and equal facilities had been provided for them. For the next sixty years, "Separate but Equal" would be the catchphrase that white supremacists would use to repress and separate black people from the mainstream white society.

But in 1896, the average American—black or white—did not typically follow the workings of the Supreme Court, and few of them saw what was on the horizon. Oblivious to exactly what was coming, Mack Mason, went on with the process of shifting from boyhood to being a man.

Mack was a fully grown young man out of his parent's house and living on his own when he met and courted a pretty nineteen-year-old named Sarah Shatteen Thompson, commonly called Sallie. His courtship was ultimately successful, and Mack and Sallie were married on December 15, 1902, in Washington County, Georgia.

Sallie Thompson had been born in June of 1883 in Washington County, Georgia, to parents Peter Thompson and Ann M. Shatteen. Sadly, Sallie's mother died when she was only five years old. Sallie's father had to work, so she went to live with her grandmother, Sallie Shatteen, for whom she was named. She was still living with her grandmother when she married Mack Mason.

By the time of their marriage, many of the harsh segregation laws that the white supremacists had been pushing had been put in place. The collection of repressive laws that forced separation between whites and African Americans in nearly every element of life became known as "Jim Crow." The name was taken from a character in a mid-1800s minstrel show in which white men would dress up in blackface and outlandish costumes and sing and dance to "colored" music. History does not record when or how the name became associated with the pattern of segregationist laws, but everyone soon knew what it meant.

And what Jim Crow meant for black people was all bad. By 1910, ten of the eleven former Confederate states had passed new constitutions or amendments to existing constitutions that used a combination of poll taxes, literacy and comprehension tests, along with residency and record-keeping requirements, to effectively disenfranchise most blacks and tens of thousands of poor whites. Suddenly, black men who had been voting for nearly 30 years were suddenly told that they were no longer qualified to vote.

The deliberate and unapologetic nature of these acts is shown by a law passed in Oklahoma. Seeing that their new anti-black laws were also causing thousands of poor whites to lose their voting rights, Oklahoma passed an incredibly cynical amendment to their new law stating that anyone who had voted, or whose ancestor had voted, prior to 1866, would be exempt from the restrictive elements of the new law. Since only white men voted prior to 1866, this amendment made all white men exempt from the literacy test and the other new requirements.

In Washington, D.C., Woodrow Wilson, the first Southern-born President since the Civil War, had apparently decided to become the "Racist-in-Chief." The Federal Government had been integrated pretty much since the Civil War. Wilson changed that by firing all black department heads, demoting a number of black military officers to noncommissioned officers, and, where black employees were not fired, segregating departments into black and white offices.

In the various states, all public facilities were suddenly made separate. From the iconic water fountains, to buses, street cars, restaurants, bathrooms, city and county parks, doctor's offices, and on and on, henceforth, some were for blacks, some for whites—none were for both.

Blacks and whites could not marry, could not share hospital rooms, could not play baseball together, could not be in the same insane asylums, and could not be buried in the same cemeteries. The goal seemed to be to make the black people invisible to white society—and it seemed to be working. The progress made during the years since the Civil War had been turned on its head. Anyone violating one of these laws could easily end up in jail . . . or worse. This was the world in which Mack and Sallie Mason began their married lives.

Mack Mason was a hard-working man who did what was necessary to provide for his family. While growing up, his only training had been in farm labor, and early in his marriage he usually worked as a farmhand. Farm work often came and went with the season, requiring the family to sometimes move to follow the work. In the years after their marriage, Mack, Sallie, and the family moved to Louisville, Jefferson County, Georgia, where they lived for many years.

Mack worked as a stable hand on a farm for a while, and then later worked for a sawmill in the same area. After the sawmill, Mack got a chance to farm for himself as a sharecropper. The farm was in Wadley, Jefferson County, Georgia, and he rented it by agreeing to share the profits of the crops that he raised. It was during these years in Washington and Jefferson Counties that Mack and Sallie's seven children were born: Jesse, John, Annie Lee, Maria, Eddie, Robert, and Melvin. Eddie—the progenitor of this line—would eventually honor his brother, Melvin, using his name as the base for his daughter's name, Melvalean.

Sometime between Melvin Mason's birth and April of 1930, Mack and Sallie moved the family to Savannah, Georgia, where Mack and Sallie lived out the remainder of their lives. Mack worked for some years in a fertilizer plant, and later got a job as a woodcutter in a pulpwood mill. It would be the job that he finally retired from.

Sallie Thompson Mason, a dedicated wife, mother, and support for her husband, came down with cancer and succumbed to it in Savannah on March 21, 1938. She and Mack had been married for 35 years. Sallie was buried in the Lincoln Cemetery, Chatham County, Georgia. Mack lived on in Savannah for another 24 years. He never remarried. He retired in the early 1940s, and lived with his daughter Annie Lee after that. Mack died in her house on September 18, 1962.

Mack had been born during the relatively brief period following the Civil War when it appeared that African Americans in Georgia were going get at least most of the rights guaranteed them by the U.S. Constitution. He went on to live the bulk of his life under the heavy weight of the Jim Crow laws that stole that promise away from them. But before he died, he got to see the beginnings of change: the rise of leaders like Martin Luther King and the passage of the first laws that would start the pendulum swinging back toward a greater freedom again.

Mack and Sallie's fifth child, Eddie Mason, is the direct ancestor of this family line. Eddie was born at a hard time for Sallie and the family. As a result, he spent most of his life being raised by willing relatives. During this period, he met an Army man named Mazo whom he came to greatly admire. [See the previous narrative fore details]

Robert J. W. Forsyth & Cressie Jo Curry

Wednesday, the fifteenth of September, 1926—the day that Robert Joseph Washington Forsyth was born as the second child of Percy Campbell Forsythe and Nina Washington—dawned hot and muggy in the city of Savannah, Georgia. Despite the fact that the first day of fall was only nine days away, summer was tenaciously refusing to surrender its hold, and the citizens of the city had resigned themselves to another day of sweating in the sweltering heat. To Robert, of course, it made little difference. It was his day and his time.

Unfortunately, it was a difficult time in Georgia. Soaring manufacturing and production were making the early 1920s boom times for much of America, but not for all. In the South, and especially in Georgia, earlier economic good times had been built on the back of a strong cotton industry. And by the time that Robert J. was born, overproduction, foreign competition, new man-made fabrics, a long drought—and worst of all, the boll-weevil—had seriously devastated Georgia's cotton-based economy.

Then in October of 1929, when Robert J. was only three years old, the financial collapse that became known as the Great Depression began and times got very hard for the entire world. Life was especially harsh for blacks, many of whom were part of Georgia's sharecropping farming culture. Unable to earn a living, many were forced off their land entirely by declining crop prices. Some took to the road, heading north into major urban areas and industrial centers. But many found themselves forced into Georgia's towns and cities, where they often competed with locals for menial jobs.

Fortunately, Savannah, as one of America's premier seaports, fared better than most of Georgia. Some businesses, such as the paper pulp and food- and sugar-processing industries that had begun prior to the Depression, were able to not only survive, but to thrive. No working man was going to get rich, but there were jobs to be had. This was the environment in which Robert J. Forsythe spent his first fifteen years

Robert's father, Percy, was one of those men who benefited from the Port of Savannah. He worked as a cook on a steamship of the Steamship of Savannah Company that hauled cargo and passengers from the Port of New York to Boston and then on to Savannah, Georgia. The ship then made the same trip in reverse with a new cargo and passenger load. The job was steady, and it probably paid better than many jobs that were available locally. But it was also a job that often left Nina and Robert at home alone for weeks at a time.

Savannah's port facilities also played a prominent role in World War II. When the war that would soon become World War II started in Europe in 1939, the U.S. started sending supplies overseas to help England. To help do this, they contracted ships belonging to the

Savannah Steamship Company. Beginning in September 1941, Percy Forsythe's ship ended passenger service began carrying only cargoes considered important to the U.S. war effort. At the same time, the shipyard at the Port of Savannah began gearing up and was soon one of the nation's most active Atlantic shipyards for the construction of Liberty Ship transports for the U.S. war effort.

At nine minutes after nine, on the evening of 19 January, 1942, Percy Forsythe's ship, the *City of Atlanta,* was about eight miles off Cape Hatteras, North Carolina, en route to Savannah, when it was torpedoed by a German submarine. The ship was badly damaged and quickly rolled over and sank before any lifeboats could be launched. Percy and forty-two other sailors died in the attack.

The death of his father at the hands of the German submarine seems to have had a major and very specific effect on sixteen-year-old Robert J. Forsythe: ten months later, Robert went to the U.S. Navy recruiting station and enlisted. He almost certainly had to lie about his age to do so.

Because of his race and his age, Robert was assigned to the Messman Branch of the Navy—which was soon retitled as the Steward Branch. At the beginning of 1942, whites were not allowed to serve in the Steward Branch, and the entire Branch was made up of black and Filipino sailors. The Steward Branch was responsible for feeding everyone on the ship, but after Robert's training and satisfaction of a required period of service, he was rated as a Stewards Mate 1st Class. Men in this specialty were essentially waiters for the officer's mess (dining room).

This should not be taken to mean that Robert had no other duties or that he never faced the dangers of war. Stewards were actually the first African Americans to see action in World War II because following Pearl Harbor the Navy was more or less in regular contact with the enemy. And every man on a ship had a battle station when the action started. Indeed, it was after several Stewards had been recognized for extreme bravery in battle that the Navy realized that it was missing a bet and dropped its ban on African Americans serving in fields outside the Steward Branch.

Following three years of service in World War II, Robert was discharged on 15 November, 1945. Undoubtedly, he, like most African Americans returning from the war, hoped to find that his service would warrant better treatment than he had experienced growing up. If so, he was destined to be disappointed.

Racially, Savannah had always had something of split personality. During the early days of slavery, the white population had shown an unusually liberal disposition toward slaves. Slaves had been allowed to have their own public church, which could be attended by slaves from all over the city—something unheard in other slave states. After the abolition of slavery, white Savannah prided itself on having a more "genteel" relationship with the black population. In truth, Savannah never had the same level of violence between blacks and whites that was found in other Georgia cities. And certainly, as the war ended in the 1940s, Savannah's business leaders wanted to show a more cosmopolitan face to the growing numbers of foreign tourists that had begun coming into America through her port. They wanted the world believe in the idea of the city's genteel view of race relations.

But while less violent and less obvious than other Georgia cities, Jim Crow still lived in Savannah's streets. Returning black servicemen often found themselves either denied the right to vote outright, or having so many roadblocks placed in their paths it amounted to the same thing. They still had to use separate facilities from whites. Black schools still had insufficient resources, and in most places blacks were still forced to sit in the back of the bus. It was a bitter disappointment; but a man had to live and had to work to do so, and Robert Forsythe got on with it as best he could.

It was during this period of readjustment that Robert met a young woman named Lucretia "Cressie" Jo Curry, and romance ensued. Cressie Jo was also a native of Savannah, having been born there on March 5, 1929, as the first child of Frederick Curry and his young wife, Elizabeth Brown.

Despite being their first child, little Cressie Jo always found herself surrounded by numerous older children. Her father, a hardworking and responsible man, had taken the responsibility for looking after all seven of his new wife's minor siblings when both of her parents died suddenly and unexpectedly.

Frederick Curry supported this crowd, along with his own increasing family, by working as a laborer in a fertilizer plant and later as a "blocker" for a shipping company, where he ran a cotton compressor—a machine for compacting the large raw cotton bales into smaller, rectangular sizes to allow more of them to fit into the available space on a cargo ship.

As each of Elizabeth Brown Curry's siblings got older, they moved out on their own or to live with one another. But while the aunts and uncles were growing up and moving out, the Curry family was having children of their own. By the time Cressie Jo was ten years old, all of the Browns were out of the house, and they had been replaced by her own sister, Nancy, and her brothers, Frederick, Jr., Frank, and Sam.

Cressie Jo was in her late teens when she met Robert Forsythe, and was only nineteen years old when they married in Savannah, Georgia, on April 17, 1948. Robert Forsythe was twenty-one years old. Robert and Cressie Jo's daughter, Delores Ann Curry, was born that same year.

As it turned out, Robert and Cressie Jo's marriage was rather short-lived. Robert had a hard time adjusting back into the City he had left as a teenager, and had encountered some hard times following his term in the Navy. And he had apparently fallen in with some reckless friends.

In January of 1949, less than a year after his marriage to Cressie Jo, Robert Forsythe was arrested and convicted of five counts of burglary. He was sentenced to spend a minimum of five years and a maximum of twenty years in the State penitentiary, and on February 9, 1949, he entered prison. It no doubt broke Cressie Jo's heart, but the long prison term also quickly resulted in the termination of Robert and Cressie Jo's brief marriage.

Shortly after the dissolution of her marriage to Robert Forsythe, Cressie Jo had children with Edward Mazo, her future son-in-law. It was an on-again, off-again relationship, with Edward and Cressie Jo living together, parting, and coming together again for several years before parting yet again.

Over the years, Cressie Jo and Edward Mazo had several children, including four daughters: Eddie Mae, Rainey, Gobbie Denise, and Selena; and five sons: Kenneth, James, Mark, Emmanuel, and Eddie. Everyone were born in Savannah, Georgia.

In the end, Edward Mazo finally left for good. This time, Cressie Jo's older sons were of an age to get work and help support the family, and she never remarried. Life in Savannah got better for African Americans: civil rights laws were passed by Congress and locally a very strong and effective civil rights movement was proving successful at moving local laws and attitudes in a better direction.

Cressie Jo spent most of her life in Savannah, Georgia, raising her children and watching them begin their own families. In 1965, she went to Philadelphia, Pennsylvania, where she had relatives, and lived there for about a year before returning to Savannah. In her last years— when her children were all grown and gone— Cressie Jo went to live with her son Kenneth in Hinesville, Georgia.

On December 10, 1998, Cressie Jo died in the Liberty Regional Medical Center in Hinesville, Liberty County, Georgia. She was buried in the Midway Congregational Church Cemetery in Hinesville.

As for Robert Forsythe, when he was released from prison he left Georgia permanently, seeking an opportunity for a new life. Apparently, he found that opportunity in Seattle, Washington, where he settled and lived out the remainder of his life. Robert Forsythe died there on November 22, 1999, and was buried in the Tahoma National Cemetery in Kent, King County, Washington, with military honors, in recognition of his World War II service. Cressie Jo Curry and Robert Forsythe's child, Delores Curry, is the direct ancestor of this family line.

Generation Four

Our Fourth Generation includes Edward and Ranie Mason, Anne and Peter Thompson, Nina and Robert Forsyth and Elizabeth and Frederick Curry of the mid to late 1800s in Georgia, South Carolina and Nassau, Bahamas.

We are of course a nation of differences,
Those differences don't make us weak,
They're the sources of our strength...
The question is not when we came here,
But why our families came here
And what we did afterward.
-Jimmy Carter

Edward Mason & Ranie Brown

Edward "Ned" Mason was born into slavery on a plantation in Washington County, Georgia, in the year 1847. He was the first child of the young couple Alfred and Hannah Mason, who had both been born into slavery themselves, probably on the same plantation where Edward was born.

Unless Edward was born during the night, Alfred would not have met his new son until he returned to his quarters after finishing his day's work. But female slaves were typically given two or three days off after childbirth, so Hannah would have had little time to welcome Edward into his new world.

Edward was followed the next year his by the birth of his brother Noah. A five-year break between the birth of Noah and the next son, Thomas, in 1853, suggests the likelihood that Alfred and Hannah lost a child or two to stillbirth or death in early childhood. But after Thomas, Edward got a new brother or sister every year or two for the next seventeen years. There was his brother James, sister Linda, brothers Andrew, Jacob, George, and Jefferson, sister Josephine, brother Alfred, and lastly, brother Cleveland, born in 1870.

As mentioned earlier, Edward and his family were part of a Washington County, Georgia, plantation. But hearing of a "plantation," we should not be too quick to visualize the estates of white-columned mansions surrounded by miles of cotton fields that were presented to us in films such as *Gone With the Wind*. According to the 1850 U.S. Census, 1,342 white families lived in Washington County that year. An addendum to that census, known as the Slave Schedule, reported that 607 of those families—46% of the white families—owned a total of 5,809 slaves. This gave Washington County a much higher rate of slave ownership than the average for the state as a whole, at 37%. There were, however, very few of the movie-style grand plantations with their hundreds of slaves. Several plantations did hold 80 or more slaves, but the average slaveholder owned between one and eight slaves. It is far more likely, therefore, that the plantation on which the Masons lived and worked was more like a large working farm.

Customs and requirements for slave behavior and treatment varied from plantation to plantation, but in Georgia many slaves were able to live in family units, spending their limited time away from the masters' fields together. Georgia slave families also frequently cultivated their own gardens, and some were even allowed to raise livestock or supplement their families' diets by hunting and fishing. Some were permitted to gather wild berries during their off-time and sell them for money, which they were allowed to keep. They were typically given Sundays off to pursue these activities. There was a payoff to the slave owner too, of course—in the form of reduced costs for feeding his slaves.

Eventually, Christianity came to serve as a pillar of slave life in Georgia. Unlike their masters, slaves drew from Christianity the message of black equality and empowerment. In the early nineteenth century, African American preachers played a significant role in spreading the Gospel in the quarters.

Regardless of the liberalness or harshness of plantation culture, one thing was pretty much constant on each plantation: every slave there was expected to work. As a very small child, Edward would have had a relatively simple life. He would have been tended to by one of older children—if there were any—or maybe by an elderly slave woman who could no longer do her usual work. The small children would have been free to play and sleep.

However, by the time Edward was seven or eight, he would have been assigned tasks that he could be expected to complete, such as pulling weeds around the house or walking down the rows of tobacco plants picking caterpillars off the leaves and stalks. When he was a couple of years older, he might have been put to churning butter and fetching eggs from the chicken pens. Unless he got assigned to a particular job, such as caring for the animals, this progression toward heavier work would have continued until his middle to late teens, when he would have gone to the fields with the other men.

Edward Mason was sixteen years old when Abraham Lincoln's Emancipation Proclamation went into effect in January of 1863. Legally, he was free as of that moment, and with so many of the white slave masters away in the Civil War, some slaves did take the chance and begin to slip away looking for opportunities to make it on their own. Most blacks, however, remained enslaved for another year or more until Sherman's march to the sea reached its goal in Savannah and the Union Army was able to put some teeth into the Proclamation. Edward was eighteen when the Civil War ended in 1865, and slavery finally collapsed everywhere across the Confederacy. He was finally and forever free—though there were times during the coming years when it may not have felt like such a great gift.

Jobs were scarce and times were hard in those first years. Much of Georgia's wealth had been destroyed by the war and the collapse of slavery. Most of the former slave owners still had land, but without their slaves, making it profitable again was difficult. This often made life hard for both the former slave owner and former slave alike. The lack of jobs and the fear of starvation made it fairly common in those first hard years for freedmen to go back to their old plantations and work the same fields they had worked as slaves.

But there were major differences now. From the end of the Civil War until 1877, the State of Georgia was under the control of the U.S. military. Troops and Union officials overseeing the civilian leadership ensured that the new laws guaranteeing the rights of the freedmen were not violated—or that they were violated less frequently. The military also set up a court of sorts where disputes between blacks and whites could be settled fairly. These courts had arrest powers, and they also dealt swiftly with any violence or retaliation done to the freedmen by their former owners.

For the first time in his life, Edward Mason had a choice as to what he would do with his life. Under the circumstances, he initially elected to continue to work at what he knew, so he went back to the fields. But now it was his choice, and he worked as a hired hand for wages. The wages were small in those first days, but he also found that his time was now his own, and when he was not working he got to decide how to spend it. And on the third day of July in 1867, Edward spent his time doing something that neither he nor anyone else had ever thought that he would be able to do. He registered as an eligible voter in Washington County, Georgia. For the remainder of his life, Edward would be one of the deciders of how he would be governed.

At about the same time he became a voter, Edward Mason met a young neighbor girl named Ranie Brown, a freed slave like himself. Edward went on to court Ranie, and the two were married about 1869. Ranie was only eighteen when she married Edward Mason.

Ranie Brown had been born in Washington County, Georgia, in December of 1852. She was the first child of George and Mary A.

Brown. Ranie's father, George, had become a sharecropper farmer within a few years of the collapse of slavery, and he and Mary built a life on the farm. Ranie was their first daughter, but she was soon joined by his sisters Rachel and Mary, and brothers Samuel, Simon, and Remus.

Ranie was barely thirteen when slavery ended, and her life on the plantation would have been very different from Edward's simply because she was freed before she became old enough for the heavy field or house work. That does not, of course, mean that she got away with not working. Like the boys, the girls were assigned tasks as soon as they were deemed old enough to perform them. Ranie would have been old enough to watch the younger children, help clean the slave master's house, churn butter, or help pick pests off the crops. Her heaviest work came later when she married Edward Mason and became the mother of twelve children.

Edward worked hard and was soon able to get his own farm on a sharecropping contract. There, his and Ranie's own family grew quickly. Their first son, George W. Brown, was born by the end of their first year of marriage, and over the next eighteen years they had ten additional children: James Mason in 1872, Aggie in 1872, Jane in 1875, Dicey in 1876, Austin in 1878, Mack in 1880, Alonzo in 1882, Janice in 1885, Ella in 1886, and Oliver in 1888.

Sometime between 1888 and 1900, Edward "Ned" Mason died in Washington County, Georgia. Some might think him lucky—he had lived to see the ending of slavery in America, he had managed his own business for his own benefit and that of his children, and he had expressed his opinion on how he should be governed through his vote. And in the end, his journey ended before the tragedy of the Jim Crow era began.

After Edward's death, Ranie Brown Mason lived on in Washington County with her children. And Ranie did live long enough to see the beginning of the Jim Crow era bring a major erosion of the freedoms won by Civil War and Emancipation. She had to watch as stores, banks, and other businesses went from being open to everyone to being for whites only. Ranie had to watch the black man lose the right to vote after forty years of voting. And she had to watch her sons walk carefully around white women, where a simple glance taken wrong could end in a lynching. It wasn't as bad as slavery, but it no longer really felt like freedom, either.

Ranie Brown Mason died in Washington County, Georgia, sometime between 1910 and 1920. Edward and Ranie's son, Mack Mason, became the direct ancestor of this family line.

Peter Thompson & Anne M. Shatteen

February of 1860 was cold in Jefferson County, Georgia, especially in the slave quarters where fires were used only on the coldest nights. It was not a particularly good place or time to be born, but here he was anyway, Peter Thompson—first and only child of his father and Polly Thompson—taking his first breath. The women who helped with the birth had gone to their cabins or to work, and her husband had also just been called to work, as usual.

Polly, though, had been allowed a few days lying-in time to get the baby off to a good start. She hugged the baby to her chest and tucked the blanket in around them as best she could. As she drifted back to sleep, she wondered briefly what life would have in store for her son. But not in her wildest dreams could she have imagined the turbulent times into which he had just been born.

Totally unknown to the Thompsons, within days of Peter's birth, Illinois lawyer and politician Abraham Lincoln would make a speech in New York City at a private college called The Cooper Union. His goal was to introduce himself to New York as a candidate for Republican nomination for President of the United States. He spoke of his opposition to slavery and to its spread into new territories and states that would be created from America's expansion into the West.

The speech would achieve his goal beyond all expectations. The *New York Times* and the *New York Tribune* both published the speech, and the *Tribune* hailed it as "one of the happiest and most convincing political arguments ever made in this City . . . No man ever made such an impression on his first appeal to a New-York audience." To top it off, just prior to the speech Lincoln had visited the photography shop of Matthew Brady and sat for a few photos. Four days after the speech, one of these photographs of Lincoln appeared on the cover of *Harper's Weekly* magazine.

Two months later, Lincoln won the nomination as the Republican candidate for President, and six months after that he was elected President of the United States. Lincoln later remarked that Matthew Brady and his day at The Cooper Union had made him President.

Back in Georgia, slaves on the plantations had still heard almost nothing about Lincoln. But soon the talk among the whites was about little else than Lincoln and his enmity towards slavery. Indeed, prior to the election, several of the slave states had vowed to secede if he was elected. By the time of Peter Thompson's first birthday, slave owners across the South were in an uproar, and nearly every slave had heard of Abraham Lincoln. Seven states, including Georgia, had seceded from the United States, and four more would soon follow.

Surviving records show that Georgia originally hoped for a peaceful and legal separation from the Union. But when South Carolina attacked Fort Sumter, on April 12, 1861, that possibility was lost and conflict was made inevitable. Georgia's governor called for volunteers six days later and the Civil War was on. Peter Thompson was fourteen months old.

Slave life during the Civil War varied widely according to location and the financial condition of the slave owner. The war did not come directly—in the form of Union soldiers—to Washington County and Jefferson Counties until well into 1863. But long before that, very early in the war, Georgians and, consequently, their slaves were being adversely impacted. With the trains blocked, most of the foodstuffs that had come into Georgia were stopped almost immediately. And with Union ships blocking all of the Georgia ports, cotton that would have provided income was stacking up on the wharves, unable to get to market.

On the other hand, slavery broke down somewhat during the war. With most of the white men gone off to war and women running the plantations and businesses, slaves used the absence of white males to secure better working and living conditions. And as Union forces made their way into the interior of the state, many slaves ran away to seek their freedom with the advancing Northern troops.

Peter was aware of none of this, of course. No doubt, short rations made for some hungry times. And his parents had some hard choices to make about whether to stay on the plantation or risk running away toward the Union troops—especially after the Emancipation Proclamation officially made them free in the eyes of the Union forces. But Peter was only two years old when the Emancipation Proclamation was issued, and for him it was all just childhood.

When Union General William T. Sherman made his famous march from Atlanta across Georgia to the sea at Savannah in November and December of 1864, the early trickle of slave runaways became a flood. Thousands of former slaves abandoned their white former owners and followed Sherman's army to actual—as well as official—freedom. Sherman's own path to the sea took him directly through Washington County, Georgia.

On January 16, 1865, General Sherman issued Special Field Order No. 15, a temporary plan that granted each freed family forty acres of tillable land and one of the many mules that had been confiscated in his march across Georgia.

No records exist to tell us if the Thompson family were recipients of land under Special Order No. 15, but for one brief, shining year in one small part of Georgia, the fabled promise of forty acres and a mule for each family of freed slaves was actually true. Unfortunately, about a year later—after Abraham Lincoln's assassination and Vice President Andrew Johnson's becoming President—Johnson terminated Special Order No. 15, and returned all of the land to the original owners.

The Civil War ended when Peter was still only five years old. Freedom of all slaves was now official throughout the land and the United States had installed a military government over Georgia and all of the other Confederate States to protect the rights of the newly freed. Special courts were established to handle disputes or legal issues between the freedmen and the whites and to assist the former slaves in getting established. For the first time, Peter's family lived in a house that they could think of as their own. As with most freedmen, Peter's family went on doing the same kind of farm work they had done as enslaved workers, but now they worked for wages. As soon as he was old enough to handle the work, Peter also went to the fields to help the family.

Both of Peter's parents appear to have died before 1880, and his siblings scattered to their own lives. By age nineteen, Peter was again living in Washington County and was out on his own. He was still working as a farm laborer, but now he was renting his own house with the help of two boarders. Among Peter's neighbors was the Shatteen family, whose daughter Anne soon caught his eye.

Anne M. Shatteen was born about 1866, in Washington County, Georgia, the second child of Mason Shatteen and Sallie Morgan.

Anne's parents had been born and raised in slavery, but slavery had finally collapsed under the Civil War and Federal law. Anne, her older sister Linnie (born in 1862), her brother James (born in 1867), and sister Lillian (1868), were all born after slavery ended and grew up on a farm obtained by their father as a free sharecropper. They grew up in the turmoil, hardships, and conflicts of the aftermath of slavery, and never knew the harsh reality of enslavement.

With her parents' consent, Peter Thompson married fifteen-year-old Anne on May 19, 1881, in Washington County, Georgia. The young couple soon set up house in the same neighborhood where they had been living. After two years together, in June of 1883, daughter, Sarah A. Thompson, was born.

Sometime between Sarah's birth and 1900, Anne Shatteen Thompson died. The records that might have told us more about Anne Shatteen's life, or that might have told us exactly how and when she died, simply do not exist for that part of Georgia in that period.

We do know that Anne's widowed husband, Peter, had to continue to work to make a living, and so her daughter, Sarah, went to live with Anne's mother. The 1900 census report shows Peter Thompson back in Jefferson County, Georgia, living with Polly Thompson. His daughter, Sarah, was living with her grandmother, Sallie Shatteen, back in the old neighborhood in Washington County.

After several years as a widower, Peter married again and had other children. He died in Jefferson County, Georgia, between 1930 and 1940. Sarah A. Thompson is the direct ancestor of this family line.

Robert Campbell Forsythe & Nina Washington

Until wealthy foreigners recognized the joy of escaping the snow and ice of winter to sit on the beach of a tropical island, the majority of common people of the Bahama Islands lived in some level of poverty. Since their discovery by the Europeans in the 1600s, many schemes had been brought to the islands in an effort to create an economy that would benefit everyone. Most of them failed and the people stayed poor.

During the early- to mid-1800s, wrecking—salvaging cargos and sometimes passengers from ships that had wrecked on the rocky reefs in the shallow waters around the islands—was a lucrative activity. Then Britain found out that some islanders were going beyond simple salvage and were taking active action to trick ships onto the rocks. The government began regulating the practice and eventually outlawed it all together.

There was a truly wonderful flurry of wealth during the American Civil War while the Confederates used the Bahamian island of New Providence as their base of operations for the blockade-running fleet. But to the islanders' great dissatisfaction, the end of the Civil War also ended the good economic times and triggered what would be the beginning of a fifty-year economic depression.

As fortune would have it, Percy Campbell Forsythe was born on New Providence in St. Agnes Parish on the outskirts of Nassau, the island's largest town. Percy was the first child of Samuel James Forsythe and his young wife, Amelia Deane. He was born on 10 June, 1879, in the fourteenth year of the economic depression engulfing the Bahamas.

Samuel Forsythe was a hotel worker in Nassau, but pay was low and the family was poor. This probably contributed to the hard times that Samuel and Amelia had with their children—in the next few years after Percy's birth, first a daughter and then a son were born, but both died before their first birthday. Finally, in 1885, another son, Samuel James Forsythe, Jr., was born and survived.

Percy grew up in a society where about 85% of the population was black. This was partially the result of Americans with pro-slave English ideals and the large number of slaves that were brought to the Bahamas with the doomed hope of keeping the plantation economy and lifestyle alive.

Others of the majority black population were the descendants of freshly captured Africans who were taken off slaver ships when Britain outlawed the slave trade in 1807. Britain required their navy to stop the slavers and confiscate the human cargoes, which they did with great vigor. The British Navy did not, however, feel obligated to haul the freed Africans all the way back to Africa. Instead, thousands of freed Africans were off-loaded onto the various islands of the British West Indies with a modicum of supplies and with the expectation that they should make do as best they could. In 1834, Britain freed all slaves everywhere in their Empire and the black majority of the West Indies were suddenly all free to seek their fortunes and grow into whatever they could be.

It is no surprise that the white business and land owners comprised the upper social class. But it is surprising that the middle class was made up primarily of light-skinned blacks and the lower class was made up of darker-skinned people. And for a long time, it was not possible for a darker-skinned person to climb out of the lower class and into one of the higher classes—it simply wasn't allowed. It wasn't the same form of harsh discrimination faced by African Americans in America under the Jim Crow laws, but in some ways it was worse. A black American, if he was careful, could improve his own economic and social position within the black community despite white discrimination. In the Bahamas during the Percy's early years, it was almost impossible for a dark-skinned islander to do the same. Under these circumstances, it is easy to see why Percy and his brother, Samuel James, decided to emigrate to America for better opportunities.

According to his own testimony on a petition for U.S. citizenship, Percy Campbell Forsythe stated that he left the Bahamas for America in about 1898. Some records suggest that Percy may have gone first to Nova Scotia, Canada, for a while before moving to Manhattan, New York, but it appears that Samuel James went straight to Manhattan. One thing seems clear: Percy was fascinated by steamships from early on. Shortly after entering America, he found a job with a steamship company, and once he reached a position he liked, he never left.

By 1914, Percy was working in a steamer sailing up and down the east coast of the United States, hauling cargo and passengers between New York and Savannah, Georgia. Percy worked in the kitchens of the ships starting as a pantry man and, over the years, he worked his way up to one of the head cook positions.

At some point—undoubtedly during one of his layovers in Savannah—Percy Forsythe met a young woman named Lula Bachelor, a Savannah native. They apparently got along well, and when his ship turned north toward New York again, she went with him. Percy Campbell Forsythe and Lula Bachelor were married on 27 September, 1915, in Manhattan, New York.

For the next several years, Lula held down the fort at their home in Manhattan while Percy sailed the seas, away from home for days and sometimes weeks at a time. In the early 1920s, he sailed on a ship called the *Cristobal*, making runs from New York to Haiti and back. Later, Percy rejoined the Ocean Steamship Company of Savannah and was soon back on the old route between New York and Savannah, Georgia. Unfortunately, Lula Bachelor Forsythe died unexpectedly a few years later in Manhattan.

Percy Campbell Forsythe continued his work on the New York to Savannah run and some years later met and married Nina Washington, another girl from Savannah. Percy and Nina had two children: Nina Forsythe, born February 24, 1925, and Robert J. Forsythe, born September 15, 1926. Marriage and family were enough to induce Percy to shift his home base from New York City to Savannah, where he could live with the family between sailings. But it was not enough to get him to give up his career on the steamships.

Nina Washington was born October 31, 1908, in Daufuskie, Beaufort County, South Carolina, the daughter of Joseph Washington and Mary Robinson. Nina was less than a year old when the family moved from South Carolina to Savannah, Georgia, where Nina grew up.

Whether he died or left, Nina's father soon disappeared from her life. But her mother, Mary, was an enterprising lady and kept the family housed and fed by running a boarding house and lunch room— she prepared more food for lunch than was needed for her boarders and sold it to the local public. Her older brother Albert, who continued to live at home until his marriage, was a blacksmith who also helped meet expenses for the family.

Nina worked as a cook's helper after she went out on her on, but she also followed in her mother's footsteps and took in boarders. That is probably how she met Percy Campbell Forsythe. With time off between sailings—while the ship was being refueled and new cargo was being loaded—he would have needed a place to stay. The combination of interest and proximity came together, and marriage occurred.

Having regularly spent time in Savannah during his employment with a company named Ocean Shipping of Savannah, Percy quickly settled into his new life there. In July of 1941, possibly with an eye toward retirement and living out his life in his adopted country, Percy filed a petition with the United States District Court at Savannah to become an American citizen.

A little over four months later, the Japanese bombed Pearl Harbor and everybody's world shifted a bit. Shortly after the United States declared war on Japan, and recognizing an immediate need for the ability to move men and materials sooner than a new Naval fleet could be created, the United States essentially drafted all major U.S. shipping into the Merchant Marine. Percy's job did not really change, except that now passenger service was sharply curtailed and priority was giving to hauling strategic materials that would best support America's war effort.

It was a necessary step, but one that turned out to be an unfortunate one for Percy Campbell Forsythe. On 19 January, 1942, his ship, the *City of Atlanta* was in the middle of a run from New York to Savannah. The ship was unarmed and had no military escorts. It was just off the coast of North Carolina, running closer to the coast than usual in an effort to reduce the likelihood of attack by German submarines. The tactic did not succeed.

Just after 9:00 p.m., the *City of Atlanta* was hit by one torpedo from the German U-Boat U-123. The torpedo was a surface runner and struck the *City of Atlanta* at the waterline. The ship quickly took on water and began to list onto its side, making it very difficult for the crew of eight officers and 38 crewmen to abandon ship. The vessel rolled completely over and went down in about ten minutes, long before any of the four lifeboats could be launched. Percy Campbell Forsythe and all but three of his shipmates were killed. When help finally arrived about six hours later, only one officer and two men were found clinging to wreckage. The officer later died of his injuries.

Needless to say, Percy's death impacted the family greatly. Ten months after his death, Percy's son, Robert, ran off and lied about his age to join the U.S. Navy. And sadly, Nina Washington Forsythe survived her husband, Percy, by only two and a half years. She died in a Savannah, Georgia, hospital on August 5, 1944. The line continues through Robert J. Forsythe, the son of Percy and Nina Forsythe.

Frederick Curry & Elizabeth Brown

Frederick Curry was born on George Washington's birthday—February 22—in 1907. It was an unusually cold winter day in Savannah, Chatham County, Georgia, where winter days were usually fairly mild.

The ninth child of Duncan Curry and Elizabeth Alston, Frederick was born into an already large and active family, with three older brothers and five older sisters: William was born first, followed by Elizabeth, Ira, Hilda (who died in infancy), Rosa Leola, Solomon, and Edmonia. And Frederick was not the last child—brothers Frampton and Charles came along after Frederick, rounding out the siblings to an even ten.

Frederick's father, Duncan, supported this large brood by doing heavy labor, first for the railroads and later on the docks at Savannah's harbor. With a little help from the older children, the family just got by.

But financial hardships were the least of the troubles for most black Georgians in those days. Those years of the early 1900s were tough, tense times for the black people of Georgia. It was Frederick's bad luck to have been born into some of the harshest of all the Jim Crow segregation years.

In September of 1906, just months before Frederick was born, three of Atlanta's evening newspapers ran featured stories of alleged rapes by black men. Whites in Atlanta went on a "revenge" spree. When the dust settled after several days of violence and bloodshed— later known as the Atlanta Race Riot—twenty-five blacks and one white were confirmed dead. Several dozens more had been injured, and sources suggested that the casualty count was actually much higher.

Six years later, in 1912, in Forsyth County, a black teenager confessed to the rape and murder of a white girl. After a week of inflammatory reporting by three county newspapers, local whites rioted against local blacks. Three black men were hanged the first night, which was followed by a campaign of terror by night riders. Black-owned houses were dynamited and black churches were burned. More than ninety percent of the black population were told, "leave or die." In the end, it was a successful use of terror to drive more than one-thousand blacks completely out of their homes and out of the county. To this day, Forsyth County is still one of the whitest counties in Georgia.

The City of Savannah was not a place where such large-scale and violent racial drama took place during those years—the first reported Savannah race riot did not happen until 1963 during the protests to end segregation. Instead, during the first half of the twentieth century, Savannah was a place where both races lived through a kind of stylized behavioral dance that was beginning to play out all over the South. The whites taught their children how to carry themselves and how to act toward blacks, to keep "the coloreds in their place" while trying to stop short of inciting a violent reaction. Black people simultaneously taught their children how to avoid eye contact, and to say "yes sir" and "no ma'am" to all whites, even those younger than themselves. They taught the children to play the part that the whites wanted to see while living their own lives the best they could.

This uncomfortable existence went on in the midst of Jim Crow segregation, and the lack of major racial conflagrations allowed Savannah to present itself to the world as a more cosmopolitan city— one that did not really have a "colored problem." But every black person living there knew how strongly racism still thrived and how it was still taking large, if less obvious, bites out of black lives. And the threat of violence, while not always obvious, was constantly there.

In June of 1914, the lives of the Curry family suddenly and unexpectedly got even harder, both emotionally and financially. Just four months after Frederick's seventh birthday, his father, Duncan Curry, died. The older children stepped up and initially took on most of the burden of earning the family living. Two of the girls worked in a local match factory and the older boys found jobs as laborers. When

Frederick got old enough, he did his part by going to work as a laborer in a fertilizer plant.

It was while working in this job that Frederick met and took a liking to the girl next door. Frederick and seventeen-year-old Elizabeth Brown hit it off and Frederick was soon courting her in earnest. Elizabeth accepted his interest and, later, his proposal. Frederick and Elizabeth were married in September of 1928.

Elizabeth Brown was born in June of 1911 in Allendale, Barnwell County, South Carolina. She was the daughter of Joseph Brown and Nancy Frazier, and the first of what would eventually become that couple's ten children. Like Elizabeth, her parents had grown up in Allendale and had made a life for their new family there.

But for much of his life, Joseph Brown earned his living as a farm laborer, and times were getting difficult for farmers in Georgia. Much of South Georgia still had cotton as their major cash crop, but then in 1915, the boll weevil hit the area, devastating crops. From there, things just got worse for the farmer—competition from new made-made fabrics, overproduction by farmers trying to make up earlier losses, and the continuing effects of the boll weevil hit the price of cotton hard. By the mid-1920s, workers like Joseph Brown were finding it hard to earn a steady living. Eventually, Joseph Brown gave up on his home town and moved his family to Savannah, seeking better economic opportunities.

Unfortunately, his timing was terrible. A little over a year after Frederick and Elizabeth Brown's marriage, the beginning of the Great Depression hit the entire country, and like millions of other Americans—both black and white—Joseph Brown found himself out of work again. By 1930, both Joseph and Nancy Brown were out of work and living next door to their new son-in-law and seven of their minor children. Frederick still had that one hugely valuable thing that year—a job.

Frederick Curry proved himself a hardworking and responsible man when he took on the task of supporting his new wife's minor siblings. He supported this crowd, along with his own increasing family, by working as a laborer in Savannah's Virginia-Carolina Chemical Company, a fertilizer plant.

The economy remained poor throughout the 1930s and real recovery did not start until the beginning of World War II. There were small pockets of improvement, though, and these small changes allowed Elizabeth Brown Curry's siblings to begin their move out of the Curry household. Some went to new marriages, some moved out on their own, and some went in together and lived with one another until the economy recovered.

By 1940, Frederick and Elizabeth were back to having only their own family living in the household. This was a good thing for the Curry's because while the aunts and uncles were growing up and moving out, the Curry family was just plain growing on its own. Frederick and Elizabeth's first child, daughter Lucretia Jo Curry, was born on March 5, 1929, but she did not stay an only child for very long. Sister Nancy was born in 1931, and brother Frederick Curry, Jr., followed on August 18, 1936.

Frederick's job with the Virginia-Carolina Chemical Company had protected his family against the very worst of the Depression—though wages and perks dropped with the economy. With the Japanese attack on Pearl Harbor and America's entry into World War II, the Virginia-Carolina Chemical Company began to expand into new fields. It went through a few corporate name changes, but operations kept growing and expanding into many divisions in several states. For Frederick, this more or less assured him of indefinite full-time employment. Toward the end of the 1930s he had been moved into a job as a tractor operator for the company's plant in Savannah. It turned out to be a position that he was to keep for the rest of his working days.

Like all families, the Curry's had their successes and their failures. After WWII, they just settled down and got on with life. They watched their children grow up and go out to seek their new lives as adults.

Neither Frederick nor Elizabeth Curry lived long lives. But in their lifetimes they had seen some subtle changes in the humiliating behavioral dance that black people were forced to perform during their long segregation. And near the end of their lives, they got to see the beginning of the end for segregation—the 1963 street protests in Savannah where black men did not step off the sidewalk to let white people pass; where black men came before the whites, not with their hats in hand or with downward cast eyes, but with their heads up. They saw black people come into the streets, not asking for favors, but demanding their rightful place in the American story. Perhaps it was enough to allow them to them see the beginning of a new future.

Frederick Curry died in Savannah on November 13, 1964, at the age of 57 years. He was buried in Laurel Grove Cemetery in Savannah, Georgia. Elizabeth Brown Curry outlived her husband by about 11 months, and died on October 16, 1965, in Savannah, Chatham County, Georgia. She was also buried in Laurel Grove Cemetery in Savannah. Frederick Curry and Elizabeth Brown's first child, Lucretia Jo Curry, is the direct line ancestor of this family line.

CHAPTER THREE: ROMANO FAMILY

I parenti sono parenti, e gli estranei sono sempre estranei.

(Relatives are relatives, and strangers are always strangers)

-- Sicilian saying

Our Romano families were from Sicily and immigrated recently to New York. We are indebted to their struggles and pain, and the ultimate triumph to bring us freedom and opportunity.

Generation Two: Romanos

These two parents comprise the Second Generation and is the starting point for the detailed biographies included in this volume. To place their ancestors in understandable location and time, the following information was compiled. The historical text that follows will give the reader a better understanding of the times, places and events each generation leading to the parents.

Il sangue non e acqua.
(Blood is thicker than water)
- Italian saying

The name Romano is literally the old Latin word for Roman. While this strongly suggests that the original family member to bear the name came from Rome, it leaves open the possible timelines for the arrival of this family line in Sicily. They may have come with the invading Roman army 22 centuries ago, or the earliest known Romano of this family may have been the immigrant ancestor, arriving in the late 1700s. The Romano ancestors lived at one point or another over the roughly 165 years of history that we attempt to track in Sicily, including

- Palermo, where the first three generations appear to have lived
- Alia, where the immigrant ancestor, Pietro Romano, was born
- Bronte, where Annetta Carmona was born
- Messina, where Annetta Carmona Romano's family died in the 1908 Earthquake
- Lercara Friddi, the town in which the Romanos lived by the late 1800s and from which they immigrated to the United States in 1914

Sitting very close to the half way point on the road running between Palermo and Agrigento, Lercara Friddi began life as a trading post in the late 1500s. The road from Palermo used to stop at Lercara Friddi. The connection to Agrigento was built during Pietro Paolo Romano's childhood.

"May you live in interesting times!" was said to be a favorite curse among the ancient Chinese. Modern Americans, with their nearly constant search for new ways to avoid boredom, often don't understand how interesting times could be a curse. But nobody ever had to explain that curse to a Sicilian. By the time that our earliest known ancestors appear in the records of the island, Sicilians had been suffering through interesting times for more than 2500 years.

To understand the character and the lives of the Sicilian ancestors, it is necessary to understand the elements that created and shaped those characters and those lives. It is necessary to understand a little of what created the place called Sicily.

Known originally as Trinacria because of its triangular shape, Sicily, with nearly 10,000 square miles of territory, it is the largest island in the Mediterranean Sea. The name Mediterranean is taken from the Latin word mediterraneus meaning, "middle of the Earth". The ancient Greeks called it Mesogeios, meaning "interior or inland." To the ancient Greeks and Romans, the Mediterranean Sea was the center of the Earth as they knew it.

The island sits just off of the southwestern tip of Italy, with less than two miles of sea, known as the Straits of Messina, separating it from mainland Italy. Note that while the northeastern tip of Sicily practically kisses mainland Italy, the southernmost point of the island is only about 100 miles from the African coast. Indeed, parts of the African country of Tunisia are farther north than the southern tip of Sicily.

To the north and northwest are Spain and France, and Italy sits to the due north. In the northeast and east lie Greece, Yugoslavia, Bulgaria, Turkey and Syria, Lebanon, and Israel; and in the southeast Egypt and Jordan, while in the south and southwest we find Libya, Tunisia, Algeria and Morocco. If the Mediterranean was the center of the ancient world, Sicily was very nearly at the dead center of that sea. It was, in simple fact, the gateway to the Mediterranean. Any society or culture venturing out into the Mediterranean seeking trade, conquest, or simply adventure would, sooner or later, encounter the island – and most of them did.

Nearly everyone who came to early Sicily really liked what they saw: a heavily forested, mountainous island with highly fertile coastal plains. The forests to provide timber for building ships, ten thousand years' worth of weathered volcanic ash to create fertile soil and short, moderate winters to provide a long growing season created a jewel to be desired and coveted by nearly all passers-by. And coveted it was, by virtually every adventuring society in the Mediterranean and in Europe as a whole. As a result, Sicily is known to modern historians as the most conquered island in the world.

Recorded Sicilian history begins with the colonization of the island by the ancient Greeks starting about 800 - 750 BC. But Greek mythology indicates that the Greeks knew about Sicily much earlier than that. For example, Homer's epic, Odyssey, has Sicily as the home of the mighty Cyclops and of the sea monsters Scylla and Charybdis.

According to the Greek historian Thucydides, when the Greeks arrived in Sicily they found three distinct groups of people living on the island, the Sicani, the Elymians and the Sicels.

The Sicani were apparently the earliest group of inhabitants on the island. Modern archaeology has shown them to be the likely descendants of cave dwellers who painted on the walls of caves in the Monte Pellegrino area near Palermo. The paintings have been dated to about 8,000 B.C. and show strong similarities to cave paintings found in Spain. This has led some scholars to theorize that the earliest Sicani came from the Iberian Peninsula.

The Elymians are thought by some scholars to have originated in the lands bordering the Aegean Sea. The ancient Greeks claimed that they were descendants of the Trojans. Their true origins are uncertain. They settled in the extreme northwest corner of Sicily, displacing the Sicani in that area and forcing them further south and inland. Despite retaining a separate language, over time, they seem to have largely blended culturally with the Sicani.

The Sicels, or Siculi, after whom the island was eventually named were the latest settlers, arriving around 1200 BC. They spoke an Indo-European language and came from the Italian mainland. The

Siculi, like the Elymians before them, displaced the Sicani, eventually settling the eastern end of the island.

There seems to have been a lot of cultural blending of these three groups, probably through intermarriage. Archeology shows almost no difference in the later settlement sites. Undoubtedly, the genes of all of these tribes can be found among the modern Sicilians.

The list of peoples that invaded and eventually took over Sicily reads like a Who's Who of the warlike peoples of Europe and Africa. The Phoenicians (known in the Judeo-Christian Bible as the Canaanites) arrived around 800 BC, then came the Greeks (abt 750-260 BC), the Carthaginians (311-241 BC) Romans (241 BC – 440 AD), Vandals (440-476 AD), Ostrogoths (476 – 535 AD), Byzantines (535 – 831 AD), Saracens (Arabs 831 – 1072 AD), Normans (1072 – 1266 AD), Angevins (early French, 1266 – 1282 AD), Spanish (1296 – 1713 (includes Aragonese), Bourbons, and finally, the Italians.

All of these conquerors left at least some impression on Sicily and its culture. But there are a few of the invaders who deserve further mention:

The Phoenicians - Their superior sea-going skills had made the greatest traders of their day and their trade routes took them to all parts of the Mediterranean and beyond. Sicily was an ideal location for establishing trading centers and the Phoenicians established several trading colonies in western Sicily, including towns that became the current cities of Marsala and Palermo. These colonies were established to promote trade and they made little to no effort to conquer their Sicilian neighbors. During this same period, however, the Phoenicians established the city-state of Carthage on the nearby African coast. The descendants of the Phoenicians and their wars with the Greeks and Romans would make their city-state world famous. And they would include Sicily in their wars and adventures for centuries.

The Greeks, unlike the Phoenicians, did not come to trade - the Greeks came to colonize and occupy new lands. In 750 BC, the Greeks were a series of city-states that some time cooperated and sometimes made war on one another. Greeks came from most of the larger Greek City-States to grab choice sites in Sicily. They settled first in eastern Sicily and spreading across the Island. Within a century, the Sicani, Elymians, and Siculi had been thoroughly Hellenized. While substantial numbers of Sicilians were undoubtedly treated as slaves, others prospered under the Greeks. Despite frequent wars with Carthage, the Greeks ruled most of Sicily for the next 3-4 centuries. Sicily became renowned as the most beautiful part of Magna Graecia (Greater Greece) and was said to have more Greek temples and more Greeks than Greece itself. The city-state of Syracuse, on the Island's southeast coast, was reputed to be the most beautiful city in all of Greece.

The Romans - had adopted much of the Greek culture themselves, felt that they could deal with the Greeks. But when the Carthaginians took Messina, the Romans decided that they could not afford having a force that powerful or that adventurous so close to their domain. So they made a temporary treaty with the Greeks in Syracuse and made war on Carthage. It took them nearly 60 years, but by 212 BC, Rome had all of Sicily as its first Province. They found that they liked owning another country and they held the island for the next 600 years.

Rome granted Roman citizenship to the inhabitants of a few of the larger cities, but overall Roman occupation cost the average Sicilian a lifetime of poverty and hard work. As a province of Rome, Sicily had to pay taxes of one tenth of its wheat and barley. Tributes were also levied on wine, olives, fruit, vegetables, and even on pasturage. On top of the taxes, the crops that the people were allowed to keep could only be sold to Rome. Cato, a Roman politician and soldier wrote that Sicily was the "Republic's granary, the nurse at whose breast the Roman people is fed." To keep the breadbasket of Rome fulfilling its role, the Romans instituted what turned out to be perhaps the worst curse that they laid on the Sicilians - the latifundia (from the Latin for "spacious farm/estate"). Roman latifundia were parceled out to powerful Romans, retiring soldiers, and, in later centuries, to the church and its ecclesiastical arms. They were usually huge estates and they were closest thing that the ancient world had to modern industrialized agriculture. Lacking the technology of the modern world, the latifundia required slave labor. They enslaved the Sicilians, of course, and when that proved inadequate, they imported thousands of slaves from their wars and conquests elsewhere. This resulted in numerous slave revolts over the centuries and in the crucifixion of thousands of Sicilian rebels. The latifundia also required large expanses of land. When the Romans arrived, the island was largely wooded. But over the centuries the forests of Sicily fell to the latifundia and to provide the wood for fleets of Rome and for wooden buildings for the city itself. Today only a few spotty forests exist on the island.

The Saracens - In 827 AD, they were replaced by the Saracens –Arab Muslims from North Africa. The Saracens ruled Sicily for just over 200 years, but they had a major impact on the island that was long lasting and overwhelmingly positive in economic terms. They removed taxes detrimental to agriculture, added an excellent irrigation system, and introduced oranges, lemons, pistachios, and sugar cane into Sicily's agriculture. The Muslims kept their religion predominant, but there was no harsh persecution of the Christians and no attempt to prevent the practice of the religion.

The Bourbons (French nobles who had taken the crown of Spain through marriage.). The Bourbons took control of Sicily in

1734, and they ruled the Island at the time that the earliest known Romano ancestor was born. They were harsh rulers who used the latifundia and the feudal system to keep the people down and in poverty. Revolutions against them were frequent and it was the excessive force used to put down an 1820 Revolt that led to the creation and spread throughout the island of secret anti-government societies – the largest of which was the Carbonari. Some historians believe that the Mafia also came out of these secret societies. The Bourbons were still ruling Sicily when Pietro Paolo Romano – the ancestor who brought the family to America - was born.

The Italians – There had long been efforts by both mainland Italians and Sicilian sympathizers to join Sicily to Italy. In 1861 a mercenary freebooter named Giuseppe Garibaldi, who had been active in the efforts to unite mainland Italy, landed at Palermo and began an invasion that led directly to Sicily being annexed into Italy. The majority of Sicilians did not accept annexation easily, but in the end they succumbed to their final conquest – they became Italian.

As a result of their history, Sicily never developed self-rule or any real sense of nationalism – it never existed as an independent country. Greece created most of the major cities as City-States, each responsible only to and for itself. It took 1500 years for the populace to unite and seek self-government. And when they did, it was too little, too late.

The Sicilians suffered oppression at the hands of a foreign – and frequently absentee king/dictator and his locally appointed officials. Governmental justice was so often non-existent or so unfair in its administration that the Sicilians essentially rejected the concept. As a result, the working class, or peasantry, developed a strong distrust of the government and of the wealthy, both foreigners and Sicilians alike.

They held the right of justice or, more frequently, vengeance to themselves. They often refused to speak to or go through governmental agencies – the rule of Omertà was in effect long before the Mafia was fully organized. Secret societies, some aimed at liberation from foreign powers and others at criminal profit, grew out of this resentment and refusal to work with foreign kings.

So did the belief that the only people to be trusted were family and friends that one knew personally. The Sicilians most often chose to depend on the people "within the sound of the bells" – the people who could hear the bells from their local church. Everyone else was a stranger. This continued to be reflected among the Sicilian immigrants - in the Little Italy section of New York; each block tended to be populated by people from a specific Sicilian village or town.

Generation Three

Our Third Generation includes Paul Peter Romano & Kathleen McCabe of the early 1900's in Italy, Ireland and New York.

Let me in, let me in,
Immigration man
Can I cross the line and pray
Can I stay another day
- Crosby & Nash

Paul Peter Romano & Kathleen McCabe

Paolo Pietro (known as Paul Peter) Romano, son of Pietro Giuseppe Romano and Annetta Pierina Camilla Carmona was born on 31 January 1911 in Lercara, Palermo, Sicily, Italy, died on 6 October 1981 in Queens, Queens, New York, and was buried on 9 October 1981 in St. Michaels, Elmhurst. Paul married Kathleen Elizabeth McCabe, daughter of Owen McCabe and Mary Smith, on 21 August 1933 in Manhattan, New York, New York. Kathleen was born on 14 July 1905 in Manhattan, New York, New York and died on 1 October 1997 in Cumberland County, Pennsylvania. Paul Romano and Kathleen McCabe had three children.

Paul Romano was 3 years old when he stepped onto American soil. Unlike some of his older brothers and sisters, he would have had virtually no significant memories of his homeland – he would grow up thinking of himself as an American. But the America – and, more specifically, the New York that he grew up in was a very different place than it is today.

The horse was just beginning to give way to the automobile and a rash of construction between 1900 and 1915 was improving living conditions by simply providing a greater selection in living space. The cramped quasi-ghettos that faced immigrants a decade earlier were certainly not gone, but housing was improving greatly. That, along with concerted efforts on the part of New York health authorities had led to a decrease in deaths from contagious diseases. But a decrease is not a disappearance – in 1914, the year that Paul Romano arrived in Manhattan, Manhattan alone had 224 cases of typhoid, resulting in 38 deaths.

Television journalist Tom Brokaw named the generation that included Paul Romano and Kathleen McCabe as "The Greatest Generation." He gave them that label because of what they lived through and how they went on to shape America.

When they were small children, the ports, and sometimes the streets, of New York were full of American soldiers – the doughboys on their way "Over There" to save Europe from the Hun in World War I. And then, from 1918-1920, the great flu pandemic struck – more than 25,000,000 people died worldwide. New York, then a city of around six million people, lost 20,000 to 24,000 residents to the flu.

As young adults, they lived through the time of the bread lines and soup kitchens of the Great Depression. More than 20% of men of working age were out of work. It was the time when wages of $1.50-$3.00 per WEEK were common – and men were glad to work for that. It was the decade that turned men into hoboes who traveled the country looking for work to feed themselves and, often their families.

In the 1940s, as their own family was starting to grow, they watched family and friends enlist in the military and go off to serve in

World War II. Paul Romano's brother Anthony Romano. He had enlisted in the Army in March of 1941, ahead of America's entry into the war. Following the war, the Romanos participated in the expansion that created the most prosperous middle class – indeed, the most prosperous country in the world. It is also interesting to consider the vast multitude of changes in the world that they saw during their lifetimes.

Paul Romano appears to have worked much of his life in the moving business – household moving. In 1930, the U. S. Census report shows him as a shipping clerking for a moving van business. In 1981, when he died, his death certificate described him as a driver for Duken Van Lines.

Generation Four

Our Fourth Generation includes Pietro Giuseppe Romano & Annetta Carmona of the mid to late 1880's in Italy.

A family without a genealogy is
Like a country without a history.
      -   Chinese saying

Pietro Giuseppe Romano & Annetta Carmona

Pietro Giuseppe Romano, son of Ireneo Romano and Felice Vitale, was born between 18 July 1858 and 1861 in Alia, Palermo, Sicily, Italy and died sometime after 1930. Pietro married Annetta Pierina Camilla Carmona, daughter of Angelo Carmone and Marianne Quintavalle on 3 August 1905 in Lercara Friddi (see marriage license on page 47). Annetta was born 18 June 1878 in Bronte, Catania, Sicily, Italy and died on 25 August 1936 in Manhattan, New York, New York. Marianne Quintavalle, mother of Annetta Pierina, died in the great Messina earthquake.

Children of this union were Rosalia Francesca Maddalena Romano (adopted the name Lillian in America) was born on 14 October 1899 in Lercara-Friddi, Sicily, Italy and died on 30 June 1963 in New York, New York at age 63; Iolanda Margherita Romano (used Yolanda in America) was born on 26 July 1902 in Lercara, Palermo, Sicily, Italy and died on 21 June 1986 in New York, New York at age 83; Ireneo Romano was born in 1905 in Lercara, Palermo, Sicily, Italy and died in 1941 in New York at age 36. Ireneo married Constance Taylor; Angelo Romano was born in 1908 in Lercara, Palermo, Sicily, Italy and died in 1985 in Delray Beach, Florida at age 77. Angelo married Yolanda Tripoda. Yolanda was born on 24 October 1915 and died in November 1985 in Delray Beach, Florida at age 70; Paul Peter

(Paolo Pietro) Romano to follow; Antonino Lindoro Romano (Anthony, Tony) was born in 1 July 1914 in Lercara, Palermo, Sicily, Italy and died 3 May 1991 in New York at age 77; Livia Romano was born on 20 December 1917 in New York and died on 4 September 1994 in Ulster County, New York at age 76. Livia married Anthony Peter Marchese.

Alia, the town where Pietro was born, perches 750 meters above sea level on the slopes of the southern hills of the Province of Palermo. It was founded in 1615 by Pietro Celesti, Marquis of Santa Croce, on the site of an ancient Spanish landed estate named Lalia which he had passed down to him through marriage.

Sitting along the ancient road between the city of Palermo and the city of Syracuse, Alia is located in one of Sicily's ancient places. There are ruins of at least two very early Muslim settlements nearby and archeological digs have uncovered coins, amphoras and other materials from throughout the Roman period. And the Gurfa Caves, dug into the cliffs above the town, show evidence of human occupation as early as 5000 BC.

Between 1848 and 1860, a desire for a unified Italy had grown and spread. In 1859, King Ferdinand of the Kingdom of the Two Sicilies died, leaving his inexperienced son, Francis as King. At the same time, a revolutionary general named Giuseppe led numerous expeditions and battles toward the goal of unification. After the annexation of the Grand Duchy of Tuscany, the Duchies of Modena and Parma and the Romagna to Piedmont in March 1860, Garibaldi and the Italian nationalists set their sights on the Kingdom of the Two Sicilies, which comprised all of southern Italy and Sicily, as the next step in their planned unification of Italy.

Garibaldi, aided by the English Navy, which kept the Bourbon King's ship's off of Garibaldi's back, landed in Sicily in May 0f 1860 with 1,000 volunteers. Soon after landing, he announced that he was assuming the dictatorship of Sicily in the name of the Victor Emanuel, the King of Sardinia. He began an assault on

Palermo on May 27th, 1860. The people rose up on both sides, with many volunteers joining Garibaldi while large numbers of peasants fought against him. Where supported, Garibaldi cheerfully accepted volunteers into his army. Where opposed, he brutally and bloodily repressed the peasant rebellions.

By September, Sicily had been largely taken, and Garibaldi turned his attention on Naples. In October, the Kingdom of the Two Sicilies ceased to exist. Garibaldi turned his conquests over to King Victor Emanuel. In March 1861, the Kingdom of Italy was formally established.

The battle was also far less costly in terms of death and destruction than it might have been had not the English bribed many of the King's senior officers to surrender without fighting. The battles for unification occurred primarily around the major cities where the King's troops were stationed. In the smaller towns and villages, the battle only came where partisan guerillas brought it.

Lying about 40 miles southeast of Palermo, Lercara Friddi sits on the slopes of Pizzo Lanzone, the 2nd highest peak (2,165 feet above sea level) of the hilly region between the Platani and Torto rivers. Only the nearby Colle Mare is higher. Like much of Sicily, the area has been occupied since ancient times. Recent archeological research found a prehistoric Sicani site just outside the present town. Lercara Friddi itself had its earliest beginnings as a trading post along the royal road between Palermo and Agrigento. In 1605, Spanish nobleman D. Baldassare Gomez de Amescua, acquired the fief through his marriage to Francesca Lercara and organized a proper village that over the centuries led directly to the present town.

It seems likely that the Romanos moved to Lercara, a town about 11 miles from Pietro Giuseppe Romano's birthplace in Alia and about 40 miles southeast of Palermo, long before the first record proves their residence there in 1905. It is also very unlikely that they were the first Romanos there. In modern times, Romano has become one of the most common names in Lercara Friddi.

As a side note, the Romanos had two notable neighbors in Lercara. One was shoemaker named Francesco Sinatra who was born in the town in 1857. Francesco moved his family to America in 1900, and it was there that his grandson, Frank Sinatra became a famous singer and actor. The second neighbor of interest was Salvatore Lucania, born in Lercara in 1897. His family migrated to America in 1907, where Salvatore changed his name, became known as Lucky Luciano, and founded La Cosa Nostra.

According to a prominent Italian editor, Lercara was located in "the core territory of the Mafia." The town lies about 12 miles from Corleone, and it was no simple whim that made Mario Puzo choose Corleone for his title character in his book, The Godfather. According to the Organized Crime element of the Federal Bureau of Investigation, Corleone sent more gangsters to America than any other place in Sicily.

By the time of Pietro Romano's birth, Lercara Friddi itself had already become a primary center of organized livestock theft in Sicily. This might be thought of as the 19th century equivalent of a hot car ring. The livestock theft ring traded in hot horses and mules, which were stolen throughout the island and then sold to the mining companies around Lercara Friddi. The leaders of this group were Giuseppe Anzalone and Antonino Petta, both sons of prominent land owning families in the area.

Interaction with the Mafia was probably not a daily thing, but there is no way that a successful businessman could have survived without at least some kind of interaction or arrangement with the local capos.

Romano family tradition is that Pietro Giuseppe Romano became wealthy as owner of sulfur mines near Lercara Friddi. This is totally possible, as there were literally hundreds of mines in the region. And there was at least one sulfur mine known as the Romano mine - the Romano mine was a partnership between a Romano family and an English company. It was a very large modern mine that utilized the latest technologies and the best mining practices. Steam engines powered the elevators that took the workers up and down the shafts, the small cars that moved the sulfur to the surface and the pumps that ventilated the mine.

As a result, the mine produced huge amounts of sulfur and during the best years, great profits. It has been impossible, however, to prove any connection between the Romano family connected to that mine and the family of Pietro Romano. The Romano Mine family appears to have lived on the Italian mainland, and while there is an excellent chance that he is related, I do not believe that he was directly connected to the family of Pietro G. Romano.

The same unstable plate tectonics that give Sicily its volcanoes and its earthquakes also deposited among the hills of the southern end of Palermo and northern end Girgenti Provinces with huge, and easily accessible, sulfur deposits. These deposits would play a major role in the social and economic development of Lercara Friddi – indeed, of Sicily, itself – for centuries.

It was perhaps both Sicily's luck and its misfortune that sulfur has turned out to be one of the most useful elements on earth. Originally called brimstone and believed by some cultures to be the fuel of the hell's fires, sulfur was not recognized or named as a separate element until 1770.

That did not, of course, keep the ancients from using it to aid in the smelter of copper or in the manufacture of bronze, or from finding a myriad of other uses for the stuff. The Egyptians used sulfur compounds to bleach fabric as early as 2000 B.C., and a few hundred years later, sulfur was crucial to the creation of certain colored pigments. The ancient Greeks used sulfur as a disinfectant, and the Romans used it in pharmaceutical applications, and when the Chinese developed gunpowder in the 13th century, sulfur was an essential component.

In Sicily, there is substantial evidence that the original settlers in the region (Sicani, Sicels, Elymians) discovered sulfur deposits near Lercara very early and that they were exporting it to Greece and northern Africa by around 900 BC. But it was the increased demand for gun powder beginning in the late 17th century and the increased need created by the Industrial Revolution in England in the late 18th century that brought prosperity to Lercara and to Sicily. By 1800,

Sicily had become the global supplier of sulfur, most of it sold through exclusive contracts with England.

Profits from the sulfur trade encouraged the development of more and more mines until the area around Lercara contained literally hundreds of sulfur mines. Large numbers of men and boys found employment in the mines. It was during this time that Lercara Friddi prospered and blossomed. It was not uncommon for newspapers of the day to refer to the town as piccolo Palermo, or little Palermo.

Over the next 100 years the demand for sulfur rose and fell many times – and with it the price. And when the price of sulfur rose and fell, so did the fortunes of those who depended upon it, from the mine owners to the workers who went down into the mines. When large new sulfur deposits were discovered in America, sulfur mining began a long, very slow slide down into extinction.

The driver saw the rider approaching his string from the side trail and flicked his stick against the shoulder of his lead donkey to keep him moving along. He nodded politely as his donkeys pulled abreast of the rider who had pulled his mule to a stop to let them pass. He did not recognize the man, but he had the look of a boss.

The rider waited patiently as he watched the pack train of donkeys loaded with smelted sulfur pass. Why not? It could well be sulfur from his nearby mine, and, if so, it had to get to the station to be hauled to the port. He waited a moment for the dust to settle and then kicked the mule into motion and rode on toward the mine.

As he rode, he briefly remembered how green and fresh these hills looked when he first saw them as a boy at his father's side. Now, so many mines had been opened in the region that it was sometimes difficult to tell where one ended and the next began. Oh well, silly to complain, even if only to himself; the sulfur had been good to him and his family.

Rounding a small hill of mine tailings – the piles of mined earth leftover after the sulfur had been smelted out – he was struck by the heavy fumes of burning sulfur. He quickly directed the mule onto another path that would allow him to approach the mine from a windward direction.

He could easily picture the scene that was producing the terrible fumes. Sulfur came out of the mine in large blocks and was piled onto a grill over the flames of a furnace. This causes the blocks to split and the sulfur, which melts at a mere 116 degrees, to stream down into waiting molds. Invariably, some of the sulfur went into the flames, making the fumes nearly unbearable. Back when he had first come to the mines, as a much younger man, he had thought he might become less sensitive to the fumes.

Arriving at the mine, he quickly moved to the entrance. Rather than the cage used in more prosperous mines, this one had a simple flat board on which he stood as he was slowly lowered into the darkness. As he descended, he noticed that the pervasive smell of sulfur being replaced by purer air. Finally, the descent halted and he stepped off the platform into a great vault from which several narrow, dark, grooved passages lead in different directions. Gleams of light and a thin smoke could be seen down some of these tunnels and he ducked and went down one low tunnel toward the light. The tunnel opened into another large chamber where groups of nearly nude men lit up by flickering candles and little lamps were loading a line of little trucks with ore. A little further along one of the little passages, he saw men boring and blasting. As the borers drove home their drills, they groaned as though in agony. The little boys who help bear the sulfur to the little trucks also groaned as they move along.

The mine owner knows that the groans are more drama that actual physical suffering, but it still adds a strange effect of misery and anguish that to the effect of the scene. And he knows that the workers are, in fact, suffering. The prices for sulfur have dropped yet again and these men are getting somewhere between forty and sixty cents for an eight-hour shift in the mine – the boys get no more than ten to fifteen cents for the same shift. Even at that, it could be worse – if prices continue to fall, it may be impossible to keep the mines open.

Shaken awake in the predawn darkness, he waited for the tremors to subside and made his way to the door. No sign of fire in the sky, so it was probably an earthquake and not the old volcano; he would look for smoke when the sun came up, just to be sure. He lit a lamp and went back to his bedroom. His wife was already up and dressed. Together, they quickly moved through the house checking the children and the house itself. No serious damage – just frightened children and a few cups rattled off a cupboard. He and his wife breathed easier and relaxed a little; they knew from the strength of the tremors, though, that it was almost certain that somewhere on people were probably dying.

It took a full day for the news of Messina to arrive in Lercara, and nearly a week longer to be sure of her family's fate. They were gone, all of them; lost to the terror of the earthquake that shook a city into fragments.

At 5:21 in the morning of 28 December 1908, the deadliest earthquake to ever hit Europe occurred in the straits of Messina between Sicily and Calabria on the Italian mainland. For a moment, it sounded like a heavy peal of thunder, and then the earth began to move. For about 35 seconds, tremors great and small rolled through Messina. For 35 seconds, the city's buildings, many of them built a hundred or more years earlier, shook and moved in ways the builders never imagined that they ever would; and the buildings began to fall. Moments later, the tsunami, a wall of water estimated at 20-30 feet high hit the coast and rolled over the lower part of the city. Because it formed in the Straits, the big wave rolled back and forth between Calabria and Sicily, striking Messina several times. When it finally withdrew, it had taken the lighthouses, most of the port facilities, large amounts of debris, and dead people with it. Higher in the city, above the line covered by the rolling sea, fires broke out and roared through the tons of wooden debris from the collapsed buildings.

Damaged railroads and downed telegraph lines hampered initial relief efforts. Initial rescue attempts came from survivors and from the sea, in the form of the crew of a civilian British ship that had managed to survive the tidal waves and keep itself from being thrown onto the rocks. These crewmen saved several children from the third floor of building that had lost its face by having the children lower string and then pull up and secure a rope. Two seamen then scrambled up the rope and helped the children to safety. The two men were then able to help more people trapped on even higher floors.

And then the aftershocks began, hundreds of them, continuing over the next several days. Buildings that had survived the initial quake fell to the aftershocks, injuring or killing rescuers looking for survivors in the rubble of the city. At the same time, a steady rain fell on Messina, forcing the dazed and injured survivors, dressed in nightclothes or whatever they could grab, to take shelter in caves, grottoes, and impromptu shanties built out of materials salvaged from the rubble of their former homes.

Rescuers searching the rubble for trapped survivors. Over ninety percent of the buildings in Messina, including all 87 churches, were destroyed. Searchers clearing rubble found trapped survivors up to 18 days after the earthquake.

Survivors awaiting transportation out of Messina – disease and conditions were a great concern and everyone knew that rebuilding would be a long, slow process. Most survivors were moved to the Italian mainland near Naples, but some went to other countries.

Months after the earthquake, survivors who stubbornly insisted staying near their old homes were living in tents or in shanties cobbled together from wood and materials recovered from the rubble.

Nations from all over the world sent help. Among the earliest to arrive were the American Battleships, the Connecticut, Illinois, Culgoa and Yankton. The ships were part of an American fleet – known as the Great White Fleet – which President Roosevelt had sent on a round the world tour as a show of American naval power. The fleet was in Egypt, for the traversal of the Suez Canal when word of the earthquake arrived. The ships named above were dispatched to Messina immediately. The crew of the Illinois recovered the bodies of the American consul and his wife, entombed in the ruins. The officers and crews of the other ships went into rescue and recovery mode.

The United States Navy provided hundreds of thousands of meals, medical personnel, cots, and blankets. When it was realized much more assistance was required in the face of the nearly total devastation, the Navy came forward with an extensive building program to provide critically needed housing. The houses built by American sailors became known as 'the American village.' The operation lasted for weeks and elicited genuine appreciation from Italian officials who had to create a somewhat delicate temporary relinquishment of national sovereignty to an American base in Italy.

The new Messina that eventually was rebuilt was a modern city, built to survive the earthquakes typical for the region. But the rebuilding was a long, long process. Fifty years after the earthquake, some people were still living in temporary shelters built in the days after that terrible event.

The specific details for the Romano family's decision to emigrate when they did are not known. The pressures were many, but it probably boiled down to simple economics. America had taken over domination of the global sulfur markets, reducing its selling price. And heavy emigration, particularly from western Sicily, had reduced the available labor force, pushing up the cost of production. For smaller mine operators, the squeeze simply became too much.

In the 10 years prior to our Romano family's emigration, more than 40 other Lercara Friddi Romano's had immigrated to America. Literally hundreds of other Lercara residents had taken the same trip. There would have been a great deal of news and substantial money coming back into the community from America, making it seem a more reasonable alternative to what was going on in Sicily.

"Papa," his oldest daughter said as they road through the streets of Palermo, "where are the chimneys? There are no chimneys!"
He glanced up at the building they were passing before chuckling. His children had rarely seen the city – and the younger children had never seen it "I had forgotten, but you are right! Most of the houses in Palermo, big or small, don't have fires. It is almost time for dinner - we will visit the Fiera Vecchia and introduce you to the economical kitchens."

The late afternoon sun was still shining brightly on the buildings facing the sun, but shadows were already forming in the narrow alleys as the stopped the buggy on one side of the square to wander about the market on foot. They stepped into instant bedlam of hurrying people, of dazzling light of the sun on white walls contrasted by the darkness of shadowed alleyways leading off the main square and of open shops not yet lit for the evening. And the noise was constant everywhere – the dull buzz of people conducting business pierced regularly by the competing calls of vendors: "Water here," "Olives", "Artichokes," "Fish!" "Look, children," the man said, waving his arm to encompass the square. "Here you can find in one spot elements of every part of Sicily."

Men, women and children by the score are everywhere, some eating where they stand, some taking food home. Small pails of gleaming charcoal bear upon their heads kettles of boiling artichokes. Steam and aroma from the cooking meats and vegetables; the smoke of lamps, candles and torches and burning fat and grease in the frying pans; escaping gases from the ranges in the "economical kitchens," from the charcoal fires, and from the coal stoves; the innumerable smells of fresh vegetables, meat, fish, both salt and fresh, cut flowers and goats, with an additional tang of cheap wine, gushing from big casks into pails and bottles in the open shops, mingle in a composite odor by no means as un-pleasant as might be thought.

The whole scene is a delight to the eye. Here is a good sized wine shop, its front entirely open, showing two rows of casks and an imposing array of copper bright as the sun; yonder a vegetable store completely covered with onions suspended in long strings, bunches and wreaths, decorated fancifully with green leaves and little rosettes. Beside us a tiny restaurant, its front all gas-range, yawns enticingly, while opposite glows the fiery eye of an artichoke man's tiny charcoal fire among the rustling strings of bulbs over the door.
Vendors of fried entrails and stomachs squat beside their frying pans and baskets, perforated ladles in their hands, exactly like our frankfurter men; while water-men with their highly colored stands full of clinking glasses swing along, bellowing cheerfully.

A man with a stand like the American quick lunch counters stood behind a narrow smoking counter full of hidden fire, bearing a frying pan on top. On his left a bowl of strong shredded cheese faced other dishes of butter and rolls. He was a very popular caterer, too, because as we watched him, a number of customers came up and placed an order. The proprietor, with a deft turn of his hand, split a roll, covered it liberally with a thick rich layer of shredded cheese, placed a few scraps of meat that he was cooking below and, deluging the whole with a spoon full or two of boiling grease served up the tit-bit to his eager customer.

They wandered about the market for more than an hour before the father led them to a small café where they took their meal. As they boarded the carriage and traveled to their hotel, he thought to himself that no matter what wonders they saw on the long trip or in America itself, they would not forget the hour in the Old Market.

Over the next few days while they waited to go aboard their ship, they saw the whole of Palermo. They saw the cathedrals and visited the theaters. They walked the docks, watching the hustle bustle of porters scurrying about with supplies and baggage, the scores of small gaudily painted boats of every color darting about like schools of surface dwelling tropical fish and the row of great black trans-Atlantic steamers awaiting the boarding of their passengers. They visited the great gardens with their golden orange and lemon trees and their beautiful fountains. And at night they sat on the veranda of their hotel overlooking the Marina, or walked the footpath of the Marina itself, listening to the gentle lap of the sea and enjoying the cooling sea airs. Then, finally it seemed, the day came; it was time to leave.

On 21 July 1914, the Romano family departed Palermo, Sicily, bound for the Port of New York on board the S. S. Martha Washington. The Martha Washington was a relatively new ship, as ships went in those days. She had been built in the shipyards of Glasgow, Scotland and launched in 1907. By the time that the Romanos boarded her, she had been making regular voyages from Trieste, Italy to Patras, Palermo and New York for eight years.

The ship was 460 feet long and had accommodations for 60 1st class, 130 2nd class, and 2000 3rd class passengers. The differences in these classes of accommodation were stark, as was the difference in their costs. First Class staterooms had all modern improvements and were located outside (to allow viewing of the sea through portholes) and amidships. First class passengers had access to the First Class Dining Room, which was well ventilated and was furnished with small tables, and where all first class passengers dined at one sitting. First class status also accorded the passenger access to the lounge and music room and to the Promenade Deck.

The Second Class passengers were accorded many of the same types of accommodations as First Class, but on a substantially less elegant scale. Their cabins were all well ventilated and neatly furnished, and rooms could be secured for two or four persons.

In these "modern" steam ships, Third Class accommodations had improved immensely over those of just a few years earlier, but none of them could be called commodious or luxurious in any way. There were large multi-berth dormitory like rooms for single men and similar rooms for single women. For married couples or passengers traveling with children, there were two, four or six berth cabins. The private 3rd class cabins were rather small, with a built in sink and berths in the form of bunk beds.

Oddly enough, the Romanos voyage was the last for the S. S. Martha Washington. World War I broke out while they were en route and the officers and crew decided to keep the ship in the New York harbor after debarking all of the passengers. A short time later, the U.S. government interned the ship, eventually taking it over and converting it to a U.S. Troop transport for the duration of World War I. Three years after the war, the ship was sold back into passenger service and once again worked in the Mediterranean waters, now renamed the Tel Aviv.

New York – Arrival in the New Land

Like most of this generation of Italian immigrants, the Romanos took their first steps onto U.S. soil in a place at the legendary intake center at Ellis Island. They were far from alone – in the 30 years between 1880 and 1920, more than 4 million Italians had come to the United States.

Ellis Island, approaching from the harbor where the passenger ships anchored. Jacob Riis, a turn of the century writer who studied and wrote widely on the immigrant's experience in America described Ellis Island this way in his book Children of the Tenement. Even though he wrote of immigrants arriving a full decade ahead of the Romano family, little had changed by 1914:

"Ellis Island is the nations' gateway to the promised land. In a single day it has handled seven thousand immigrants. "How much you got?" shouts the inspector at the head of the long file moving up from the quay between iron rails, and, remembering, in the same breath shrieks out, "Quanto monèta?" with a gesture that brings up from the depths of Pietro's pocket a pitiful handful of paper money. Before he has half of it out, the interpreter has him by the wrist, and with a quick movement shakes the bills out upon the desk as a dice-thrower "chucks" the ivories. Ten, twenty, forty lire. He shakes his head. Not much, but-he glances at the ship's manifest-is he going to friends? "Si, si! signor," says Pietro, eagerly. The inspector stuffs the money back in the man's pocket, shoves him on, and yells, "Wie viel geld?" at a hapless German next in line.

Newcomers were numbered, sorted, and sent through a series of inspections, where they were checked for physical and mental fitness and for their ability to find work in the U.S. The consequences of failing an eye exam, or of seeming too frail for manual labor, could be devastating; one member of a family could be sent back to Italy, perhaps never to see his or her loved ones again, because of a hint of trachoma or a careless inspector. Although less than 2 percent of Italians were turned away, fear of such a separation led some immigrants to rename Ellis Island L'Isola dell Lagrime—the Island of Tears.

Even for those who made their way successfully through the battery of inspections, Ellis Island was generally not a pleasant experience. The regulations were confusing, the crowds disorienting, the officials rushed, and the hubbub of countless competing languages must have been jarring to the nerves. The moment of departure, when successful immigrants boarded ferries for New York City or destinations further west, came as a tremendous relief. "

The Romanos, of course, came to America better prepared financially than most immigrants from Sicily. A review of the S. S. Martha Washington's passenger manifest reveals that the majority of the Romanos' fellow passengers reported between the required minimum of $50 and $100. Pietro Romano reported that he was arriving with $600 in cash - worth about $19,000 in today's money. But the rest of the experience would probably not have been much different for them.

On the day that the Romanos debarked into Ellis Island, Germany declared war on France, opening what would become World War I. The front pages of the newspapers blared stories of these world events and of an on-going Wall Street financial crisis. While these crises would eventually touch millions of American lives, in August of 1914, they were of less importance to the Romanos than finding a place to live.

The largest portion of the turn of the century Italian immigrants moving into New York City elected to settle in the numbered streets of Little Italy; later immigrants went there or moved into east Harlem. In both neighborhoods, they clumped together, with each block housing its own village from the old country. This new living environment was something of a shock to the new immigrants. People who in Italy may well have slept in small cramped houses, routinely spent most of their waking hours outdoors, socializing, working, shopping, eating. For these people, the tiny apartments in Little Italy provided a closed, claustrophobic existence - and immense hardship.

The Romanos appear to have largely avoided this experience. By 1920, the family was living in lower Midtown, on East 42nd Street, Manhattan. None the less, nearly all of their neighbors were Italians, with a Portuguese family thrown in here and there.

It is interesting to note that on the second page of the S. S. Martha Washington's manifest the family claims that they are going to New York to join Pietro Romano's brother-in-law, Luigi Mavaro. Luigi Mavaro is said to live at 92 Lexington Avenue, New York, New York. A quick check of passenger lists shows that Luigi Mavaro, of Lercara Friddi, Sicily, arrived in New York on 17 January aboard the S.S. Principe di Piemonte. On the passenger manifest, Luigi Mavaro reported that his closes living relative back in Sicily was his wife Rosa Ferrara, who lived in Lercara Friddi.

By 1920, Luigi Mavaro and family are living at 1488 Fifth Avenue, Manhattan. Luigi's occupation is reported as "Regulator" of pianos. It is almost certainly not a coincidence that his "brother-in-law", Pietro Romano is working in a piano factory that same year. It is unknown as to how Luigi Mavaro would fit the relationship of brother-in-law, but it is clear that he is a man from the old hometown back in Sicily and that Pietro Romano knew him well.

Pietro Romano was working as a laborer in a piano factory and the oldest daughters, Lillian and Yolanda, were working as dress beaders – they sewed decorative beads onto dresses. This may have felt like something of a comedown for the family, and especially for Pietro Romano, from the days when he owned the sulfur mine and employed others to work for him.

In 1920, the Romano family lived at 241 East 42nd Street, a couple of blocks east of Grand Central Station

In 1925, the New York City Directory reported Anna Romano as still living at 241 East 42nd Street, but now as a widow. By 17 April 1930, when the 1930 U. S. Census was taken for their neighborhood, the Romano family had moved from 241 East 42nd to 179 East 96th Street. Pietro Romano, father of the family, was not with them and Anna Carmona Romano was again reported as a widow. Details of exactly what became of Pietro Romano are unavailable from independent sources.

The census suggests that he died, but there is no death certificate in Manhattan for him. Family stories say that Pietro Romano was actually deported for attempting to kill his wife. In the end, both stories may be true. Pietro Romano may have returned to Sicily and died there by 1925.

By April of 1930, the Romano family had moved to 179 East 96th street, a few blocks east of Central Park. In 1930, Anna Carmona Romano was reported as head of house with no other occupation. The two older girls, Lily and Yolanda were still working as dress beaders. Kenny (Ireneo) had taken a position as a chauffeur for a private family, Angelo was a shipping clerk for Silverman's Store, and Paul was a shipping clerk for a moving company.

Beginning in the late 1920s, all of the Romano sons began the process of becoming naturalized citizens. By 1940, all of them had filed the final Petition of Citizenship. You can see copies of these petitions in the section "Some Romano Family Records' later in this document.

Generation Five

Our Fifth Generation includes Ireneo Romano & Felice Vitale of the early 1880's in Italy.

La connaissance du passe est la cle pour ourvrir l'avenir.

(Knowledge of the past is the key to opening the future)

- Marc D Thompson

Ireneo Romano & Felice Vitale

Ireneo Romano, son of Giuseppe Romano and Angela di Simone, was born on 2 December 1820 in St. Agata, Palermo, Sicily, Italy and died in Sicily, Italy. Ireneo married Felice Vitale about 1857 in Sicily, Italy, daughter of Erasmo Vitale and Maria Viviano. Felice was born on 16 November 1828 in St. Agata, Palermo, Sicily, Italy and died in Sicily, Italy.

The known children of Ireneo and Felice Vitale are Pietro Giuseppe Romano was born between 18 July 1858 and 1861 in Alia, Palermo, Sicily, Italy, and died after 1920, probably in Sicily, Italy and Carlo Romano.

Ireneo Becomes an Orphan. Giuseppe Romano dies on 25 August 1823; his death is recorded in Santa Cristina parish, Palermo, Sicily. Angela Di Simone dies on 25 January 1825; her death is recorded in the parish of Brancaccio, an early Palermo suburb.

At age 5, Ireneo Romano finds himself an orphan. It seems most likely that he was taken in by family – grandparents or an aunt of uncle, but no details are known.

The young Sicilian had been lulled almost into a slumber by the warmth of the morning sun and the movement of the carreto. He was snapped into alertness when his cousin muttered a curse and jerked the little cart to a halt. Glancing up, he saw that a man had run out of the alleyway and almost into the path of the mule. Now he watched him run into the dockyard and attempt to hide among the cargo waiting to be loaded onto the ship. A moment later, four campieri charged out of the alley and followed the man into the yard. All four men were armed with heavy cudgels and long knives; one carried a pike. The watcher thought that he recognized at least one of them as Don Niccolosi's man.

For a few minutes, the running man made a game effort of it as he dodged about trying to keep casks and bales between him and the campieri. The outcome was never in doubt, of course, and the only question in the young man's mind as he watched from the cart was whether the man would be merely beaten within an inch or his life or killed outright. The answer came quickly and the man lay bleeding on the ground. One of the campieri retrieved a bag from the felled man and the four walked back toward the cart and the alley from which they had come. As they passed the cart, one of the campieri hoisted the recovered sack and said "He stole oranges."

As the men disappeared down the alley, his cousin started the mule on its way. The young man on the cart said nothing, but he glanced once more at the man on the ground. At most, the sack; could have held 10 or 12 oranges. Just one of Don Niccolosi's trees would produce hundreds of oranges each year and for a dozen, the man had been killed – or at least nearly so. He shook himself as if to clear his head. That was foolish thinking. The first lesson to take from this was that the man was a great fool to risk his life for so little potential gain. The second lesson was that he would take care not to cross Don Niccolosi.

In 1825, King Ferdinand dies and his son, Francis succeeds him. Just five years later, King Francis dies and is succeeded by his son, Ferdinand II. During all of this, very little changes for the Sicilians. Soon the hostilities toward the King's government resume and so do the executions. The overwhelming suppression has an effect; there is little open rebellion, and little organization among the Sicilian rebels.

Cholera! The Cholera epidemic that has been terrorizing Europe is loose in Sicily and people are dropping faster than they can be carried away. The young man did not know what to do or how to act. He found it hard to fear an unseen threat, but very easy to fear the sight of carts full of the dead being moved down the city streets. But now Uncle Paolo had decided it was time to flee. Now they were preparing to flee.

"Dress in rough clothes, work clothes," his uncle ordered. "The damned superstitious peasants have gone insane. They think that the epidemic is some evil worked on them by the government and the rich. They have been killing the government workers sent to aid them and Antonino to me that they had even stoned the Sisters of Charity while they were visiting the sick and dying. He says that even wearing a decent coat will earn you an attack"

The carts are quickly loaded and they take to the road. They are going to a cousin's house in Alia a small town in the mountains southeast of Palermo. Uncle hopes that the cooler climate and fewer people will give them a better chance of escaping the cholera.

Six weeks later, it is clear that the flight to the mountains has not worked; nearly half of the population of Alia has died. The young man has worked with the men of Alia to bury the victims of the epidemic. At the height of the deaths, they had no time for ceremony or individual graves. More than 300 of the cholera victims went into a mass grave. It is a memory that will stay with him forever.
Before the end of the year, it is estimated that about 25% of the population of Sicily has died.

The revolt against the government that started with the peasant reaction to the cholera has turned into a full political movement and the authorities in Naples and their Austrian allies have suppressed the movement with a ferocious vengeance. Even the most trivial suspicion of liberalism is enough to get a man imprisoned, flogged and tortured.

For the first time ever, the major Palermo and Messina come together in their disdain and in their conspiracy's against the king. In a September 1847, a peasant rising in Reggio Calabria spread across the strait to Messina, stimulating even more unrest in Sicily.

Despite everything, life goes on apace. Children grow into men and women, old people die. The seasons pass with crops planted and harvested. The ships come and go at Palermo. It is a time of relative peace, but through it all, the Sicilians continue to chafe under the Bourbon rule.

In Palermo on January 9, 1848, a veteran of the 1820 revolution named Francesco Bagnasco released a pamphlet that called for an uprising on the King's birthday. Sicily took him up on it with a passion. The radicals, who initiated the rising, were seeking autonomy and constitutional government. The peasants and urban poor thought little of constitutionalism. They would fight for more basic reasons; they would fight for land and work.

The streets of Palermo started to fill almost immediately in response to the call to arms and by the twelfth, the birthday of King Ferdinand, they were packed. The revolution was on.

Buoyed by the initial success of the Sicilians, Neapolitans rebels also took up arms. Pressure from both sides influenced the King to buy himself time by granting Sicilian demands – he reinstated Sicily's constitution and reconvened a Sicilian parliament. For about a year, Sicily reveled in new-found freedom.

But with the help of loyalists in Naples, by the end of the year the King quelled his threat at home and turned his attention on the Sicilian rebels. As usual, it was

Palermo that had been the instigator and it was Palermo that bore the brunt of his retribution. Rather than confront the rebels in the tortuous streets of the hostile city, the army decided to bombard Palermo from the fortress of Castellamare. The bombardment laid waste to much of the City. The people tried to surrender, but the King ignored them. The bombardment continued for two days after the rebels surrendered. That week, the King earned the name that would follow him through history – King Bomba.

When it was all over, the young Sicilian walked through his neighborhood, hardly recognizing the familiar old streets. Too much. This was just too much. Maybe it was time to leave Palermo and join his cousins inland.

First light was just breaking as he harnessed the donkey to the old carreto. As he worked, he quickly studied the little cart with a practiced eye, checking the wheels and the key joints. The carreto was old, but still sturdy – he had put on new wheels just last year. And if this year brought a good harvest, he would have the fading side paintings restored. The paintings were of the famous scene where St. Agata saved her town from the lava flow of one of Mount Etna's more or less regular eruptions by laying her sacred scarf in the path of the lava. Getting the paintings restored would be appropriate this year. The constant pillar of smoke in the east told him that the ancient volcano was showing its anger once again.

His inspection complete, the man loaded a little packet of food and his water bottle into the cart along with a few tools before leading the donkey out into street. The clangs and thumps drifting to him through fresh morning air told him that the village of Alia was stirring, but a quick glance around revealed no one else on the street. That was okay with him; he enjoyed being the first one out. There would be less dust on the road to the fields. He mounted the cart and twitched the reins to start the donkey down the road toward his new fields.

Like the peasant farmers who actually worked his lands, he and his family lived in town, while most of his fields lay some miles away in the little valleys. He liked living in the city and when he went to the fields, he usually enjoyed the long, slow morning ride. A man could think out here, accompanied only by his own thoughts and the occasional song of a goldfinch from the fields that he passed. And today he had much to think about. He needed to start the Inquilini to work on the 200 acres at the top of the valley

As he cleared the first turn in the road, he saw that he was not the first out after all; there was a small group of laborers walking down the road ahead of him. As he got closer, he saw that he did not know them. Had they been his men, he probably would have offered them a ride. Since they were not, he nodded to them and continued alone. It never occurred to him to offer them a ride and it never occurred to the men to expect the offer of one. After all, he was a Borgesi and they were Contadinas and among the three general classes of farmer in Sicily at the end of the 18th and throughout the 19th century, the Borgesi were at the top and the Contadini were at the bottom.

Borgesi like him were the middlemen; they leased large sections of land from the absentee land owners, rented plots of it to tenant farmers, and farmed the remainder themselves. On the land they held to themselves, they tended to be managers who only very rarely actually worked the land. The Contadini, on the other hand, were the wage-earning field workers on the farms of Sicily. In the common vernacular, the differences between the farming classes were often reduced to the "caps", the workers, and the "hats", the bosses.

The Borgesi smiled to himself, knowing that he had been lucky. It had by no means been assured that he would succeed in his role when he had first moved from his job as a sort of junior merchant in the family business to active management of the land. He had missed the activity of the city at first, but he was happy being the middleman now. By being stingy with his earnings and with a small inheritance from his father and his uncle, he had been able expand his holdings.

These little two wheeled wagons were the standard form of transportation for working to middle class Sicilians well into the early 1900s. Families with more money might have two carts, a carreto del lavoro (work cart) and a carreto del gara (for parades and ceremonies such as wedding and religious festivals).

Peasant farmers who worked the land, but never owned it, lived in towns that were often many miles from the fields that they worked. During busy parts of the season, it was common for them to build straw shelters where they would sleep during the work week before returning to their homes on the weekend.

His current leases were mostly in almonds and in olives and carobs. He would love to have wheat fields, but none of his leaseholds were big enough to make wheat profitable.

But now his cousin was after him to go partners on some new lands that were nearer to Lercara than to Alia. There was even some talk of taking mineral rights on the land and mining the sulfur themselves. And if that didn't work out, he felt pretty sure that he could contract more land in that area when it became available. His family was prospering – and a good thing, too, with a new son in the house. If things continued to go well, it would be another good year.

Generation Six

Our Sixth Generation includes Giuseppe Romano & Angela di Simone of the late 1700s in Italy.

There is a history in all men's lives.
- William Shakespeare

Giuseppe Romano & Angela di Simone

Giuseppe Romano, son of Antonio Romano and Maria, was born about 1780 in St. Agata, Palermo, Sicily and died on 25 August 1823 in St. Cristina, Palermo, Sicily. Another name for Giuseppe was Joseph Romano. Giuseppe married Angela di Simone, daughter of Antonio di Simone and Unknown, in Sicily in about 1815. Angela was born about 1792 in Italy and died on 20 January 1825 in Brancaccio, Palermo, Sicily, Italy.

The known child of Giuseppe Romano and Angela di Simone is Ireneo Romano was born on 2 December 1820 in St. Agata, Palermo, Sicily, Italy and died in Sicily, Italy.

The afternoon sun slanted down over the rooftops of nearby houses and here and there in Palermo small groups of men sat on the porticos, sipping coffee and talking business and politics. The major topic was the fact that the King and his sizeable retinue was returning to Naples. They had been a little worried over the potential ill effects of the presence of so many foreign troops. But the last four years had been easier than any of them had expected.

The King and family were rarely seen in Palermo. They had spent most of their time at the Chinese Villa which was built in a park at the foot of Mount Pellegrino, or at the Royal Hunting Lodge on his estate in the mountains near Corleone. And no one could complain about business; trade had been good with the increased visits from the English fleet. So now the conversation was about what might happen when the King returned to Naples. The pessimists said that business would slow. The realists said wait and see.

Just as surely as the summer brings the hot sirrocco blowing out of Africa, in Sicily the son follows the father into the family business. And it has been a good year for trade in Palermo. The Americans came seeking allies against the Barbary pirates. Sicily, who also lost ships and goods to the priates, joined the coalition, along with the Swedes, Maltese, Portuguese, and Moroccans to patrol the Mediterranean and interdict pirate actions. Not only did Palermo benefit from the better flow of trade goods, but they also made profits from supplying the fleets.

The young man stood near the warehouse door and watched as the ship unloaded soldiers and officers. It was an English ship, here, he had heard, to advise and support King Ferdinand in his argument with Napoleon. Apparently Napoleon had stopped playing and had sent his army south to conquer Naples and to install his brother on the throne.

Now, the English have once again rescued King Ferdinand and brought him to his palace in Sicily. Once again Ferdinand has brought his Neapolitan guards, along with a much larger band of ruffians. This time there is a much stronger contingent of the English Navy, too.

After the initial excitement, life settles into a pace not much different than before.

God bless the English Navy! The King cannot survive without the support of the English and he knows it too well. The English Minister, Lord William Bentick, has used this fact to pressure the King into approving an English Style Constitution for Sicily! There will be a representative Parliament, a real parliament, not that feudal facade of a parliamentary system that had existed in the past. Finally, Sicily's life and future will be in the hands of Sicilians!

Today, King Ferdinand personally opened the first session of the Sicilian Parliament. For the first time ever, Sicilians have a strong voice in their governance. There is much joy and celebration in Palermo.

The Austrians have defeated the French and have restored King Ferdinand to his throne in Naples. He has proclaimed himself king of the Kingdom of the Two Sicilies and has proclaimed that legislation and administration will be uniform throughout his Kingdom. He has destroyed the Sicilian constitution in all but name. Anger and frustration is everywhere in the streets of Palermo. The people want revolution, but for now cooler heads prevail. Diplomacy will get its chance.

Meanwhile, daily life goes on; young men court and marry, children grow, business gets done.

The military in Naples have revolted and forced the King to institute the Spanish Constitution of 1812. They have declared a united parliament for both Sicily and Naples, to be held in Naples. Sicily's parliament has rejected this outrageous proposition and has demanded that the King's union of the two kingdoms be repealed and that Sicily retain its right to its own parliament. The Neapolitans have refused. What now of Sicily's Constitution, Sicily's Parliament? Sicily has had representation for such a short time! But it has already grown precious and it will be retained! If doing so requires revolution, so be it.

At the end of July, Palermo declares Independence. Negotiations, small uprisings and skirmishes occur throughout August. At the end of August, 7,000 Neapolitan troops landed to enforce negotiations. One of the demands by the Army was that the Neapolitan forces occupy Palermo and that the Parliament be convened. The Parliament would then decide the question of independence. The Sicilian negotiators agree – but the people of Palermo do not.

The troops move on Palermo, but the people rise up against them fighting them in the streets. For days, the people seem to be winning. But on the 26th of September, the Neapolitans attack again, sacking and burning houses in the suburbs; murdering the inhabitants. The mob in Palermo retaliates by killing Neapolitan residents of

Palermo and any who support them. That night, the Neapolitan fleet and the fortresses at Castellamare and Garita bombard the City with cannon fire as the troops capture the suburbs and began to slowly penetrate into the heart of Palermo. It is estimated that about 500 of the Neapolitans are killed that day and night – but about 4,000 Sicilians are killed. Within a few days, the populace is forced to surrender Palermo to the King's troops.

In the end, the revolution has been bitter and short with much destruction in the streets of Palermo. Hundreds of houses are destroyed along with businesses, libraries, and lives. And in the end nothing is gained. The Neapolitans want representative government for themselves, but not for Sicily. Their soldiers support the King against Sicily and there has been much bloodshed and destruction in the streets of Palermo. Hundreds have been arrested and executed. What a year for a son to be born.

Now the Neapolitans know how Sicily feels; their freedoms and Sicily's are all down the same hole. The Austrians have marched on Naples in support of King Ferdinand. All constitutions are abolished and the King is returned to absolute power. It is hard not to feel that the Neapolitans had it coming, but it is a black time for all.

The damage that the revolution had done to Palermo is slowly rebuilt. The carretas of Palermo take produce and goods to the port for shipping and receive other goods for delivery to the shops of Palermo and nearby towns. Business gets done, children grow, old people die; life goes on.

Politically, the concentration of power in the Kingdom of the Two Sicilies becomes even more concentrated in Naples. In Sicily, the anger of the people continues to fester and grows among the people. For the first time since in history the great city states of Sicily begin to join together in a national undertaking. A conspiracy begins to grow, a conspiracy against the King and the Neapolitans.

Spies tell the government in Naples about the plots; whenever there is a whisper that something may actually happen, the King's officers crush it with ruthless violence. In 1823, 3 men from Palermo and six from Messina are condemned and shot. Nine more are executed for a plot to poison bread and wine being delivered to the Austrian soldiers occupying the island.

Generation Seven

Our Seventh Generation includes Antonio & Maria Romano of the mid 1700s in Italy.

The generations of living things pass in a short time,
And like runners hand on the torch of life.
-   Lucretius

Antonio & Maria Romano

Antonio Romano was born about 1750 in Italy and died in Sicily, Italy. Antonio married Maria before 1780 in Sicily, Italy. Maria was born from about 1750 to 1765 in Italy and died in Sicily, Italy.

The known children of Antonio Romano and Maria are Giuseppe Romano was born about 1780 in St. Agata, Palermo, Sicily and died on 25 August 1823 in St. Cristina, Palermo, Sicily and Angela Romano was born about 1781 and died on 20 January 1825 in Brancaccio, Palermo, Sicily.

The boy stood quietly to one side and listened to the older men talking business and politics. Ordinarily, this bored him and he would busy himself looking to see if what new thing that the nearby shops might have to offer. Today, though, his attention was caught when he had heard his father say "A boy? How can a boy of eight be king?" That got his attention; he was only 8 years old himself. He stepped a little closer.

He did not quite understand why, but apparently King Charles had returned to Spain forever and he had left his young son Ferdinand behind to be the King of Naples and Sicily. It was an astonishing idea that sent his thoughts swirling. Could a boy be king? Could he, who was the same age as this new king, and maybe even a little older, see himself as a king? Never in this world. And to be left behind by a Papa who went away forever? Unthinkable. He thought that, perhaps, he might feel a little sorry for this new king to be facing such a strange new life without even his papa to comfort him. It was not the last time that the young man would think of the King, but it was the last time that he would feel sorry for him.

Young Romano sat on a rock at the top of the road leading down into Palermo and smiled down on his city. It was true, he thought, that Palermo from afar was strikingly beautiful, regardless of whether you approach from the mountains or the sea. From the sea, these mountains that he currently looked down from rose verdant and green behind the city, while east and west of the city, Monte Pellegrino and Monte Catalfano, respectively, extend into the sea, creating the harbor that first drew the Phoenicians to settle there.

But from here, from above, you could see the natural bowl created by the mountains rising on three sides of Palermo, the fertile coastal plain around the city feed massive groves of oranges, lemons, almonds, peaches and plums. From here, you could understand why some long ago traveler saw this view of Palermo and seeing an inverted seashell rather than a bowl, gave the area its nickname: la Concha di Oro – the Golden Conch.

Looking at his city from this vantage point, the young Sicilian saw both the wisdom of the ancients who first laid out Palermo and the much less organized way the City had evolved over the centuries since. The first two major streets, the Corso Toledo and the Via Maqueda (later called Nuova Strada) paved, like nearly the entire city, with large blocks of dressed lava taken from the ancient eruptions of Mt. Etna, still defined the City.

From his seat, he could see the full length of the Corso Toledo, running from northwest, where the City's main gates open to the sea shore, to the southeast where it ended near the King's palace. In the middle of the city, the Corso Toledo intersected the Via Magueda, the major east- east-west street at the Piazza Vigliena. The piazza, more commonly called the Quattro Canti (Four Corners), was formed by a large Greek style building on each corner and a fountain with statues that stood in the square itself. He could remember standing in the Quattro Canti as a boy and realizing that he could easily see all four city gates, each of which lies about a half mile from the Piazza.

His eyes moved to the Marina, a long, attractively planted park just outside the City's main gate at the north end of the Corso Toledo. Averaging about 80 yards wide and measuring about a mile long, the park ran east to west between the city walls and the sea. There were a few people on paved footpath running the full length of the beautiful promenade along the water's edge, but no carriages on the parallel roadway nearer the city wall. The people of Palermo preferred the Marina at night when the cooling breezes from the sea were a relief from the warmth of the city.

His seat was restful and white Palermo was beautiful against the blue-green sea beyond. But it was, time to be on his way. He slid easily from his seat and began his walk down into the city that he had been admiring. Entering Palermo, Antonio found the Corso Toledo as it nearly always was - crowded with people on the move, giving one an almost constant sense of motion. Nearly every house, even the grander ones, seemed to have an open shop or cafe as its ground floor. Above the shops were living quarters, and nearly every house had a wooden balcony.

The people that he passed on the streets were an interesting mix. Palermo's busy port made Palermo Sicily's largest and most cosmopolitan city. It is not only Sicily's primary port, but is also one of the more significant Mediterranean ports.

As a result, the Romanos of Palermo had the opportunity to a meet and know a surprisingly wide array of peoples: Europeans from almost every country, Maltese merchants, Muslim traders from Tunis, Egypt and other nearby African neighbors, as well as Greeks and visitors from the Balkans. The Englishmen initially came seeking trade and brought along the English navy with their ships of war to protect the English traders and generally harass England's enemies of the moment. And from even much farther away, there were the Americans.

While we cannot be absolutely sure, it appears that the Romanos probably lived in the southeastern quarter of Palermo. Certainly, the small church of St. Agata (in the top circle), where the births or deaths of several Romanos were recorded, sits on Via Espero, a little south of the Via Maqueda and not far from its eastern gate, which is known as Porta Santa Agata. The Chisea di St. Cristina (lower circle), another church with Romano records, was located several blocks to the south of St. Agata. Brancaccio, where Angela di Simone Romano's death was recorded, is just off this map to the southeast (lower right).

Stepping off of the wide primary road Antonio soon found himself in the labyrinth of narrow, crooked streets common to virtually all European cities that had evolved over the centuries. It is here that he encountered the phenomenon called "shirt scenery," where, the laundry of Palermo hangs on lines running across the streets and fastened between balconies or poles arranged in a "picturesque intricacy of effect and play of light and shadow and color, which in its way is remarkably striking."

Antonio Romano's Palermo was also a Palermo chafing under the rule of the most recent King. Under the previous centuries of Spanish rule, Sicily and particularly Palermo, was governed by a Viceroy appointed by Spain. This system allowed Palermo at least a modicum of power and a say in how things ran on the Island. When even this small power of was lost under the rule of the Bourbon Kings, the Sicilians grew resentful. This unrest was to eventually have an impact on Antonio's life and on the lives of his children and grandchildren.

He sat quietly on his balcony, watching activity on the street. It was the most amazing sight – perhaps among the oddest spectacles Palermo had seen. Hundreds of Sicilian peasants and day laborers were marching through the streets to the Bishop's house shouting and chanting as they went. They had come to complain about the religious trial ritual known in the Church as the Spanish Inquisition. At first, the young Sicilian was not surprised – news that the King Ferdinand was abolishing the horrific practice had spread rapidly and most Sicilians bade it good riddance. During all the years of Spanish rule, the Inquisition had taken a heavy toll on Sicilians, especially the educated or those with a little money in their pockets.

To the watcher's surprise, this crowd was not protesting against the Inquisition. Instead, they were demonstrating to demand that the Catholic Church NOT end the Inquisitorial Courts. The working class wanted the right for the public torture and burning of heretics and witches to continue; they demanded the right to keep what they called "their justice."

Sicily had few Protestants or hidden Jews to persecute, so the Inquisition was perhaps even more corrupt than in other jurisdictions and was often used to control the Sicilian nobility. Indeed, the Church did not fund the Inquisition, so the Inquisitor Court's only source of income was the confiscation of the property of the condemned. As a result, it is not too surprising that a high percentage found to be guilty of heresy were from the rich land owners and the island's intellectual class. And since it was very rare when an uneducated laborer was put to the Inquisition, it was really little wonder the peasants and the day laborers supported it.

This painting is a representation of an auto-da-fé conducted in front of the Bishop's house and the Palermo Cathedral in 1724. A Priest and a nun who followed forbidden branch of Christianity called Molinists were strangled and then burned at the stake. The Molinists were trying to understand the varieties of God's knowledge, which was considered sacrilege by the mainstream of the Church.

The first small tremors shook him awake as they ran through the earth beneath Palermo, rattling the windows and the dishes in the cabinets. Like nearly all of Palermo, he leaped from bed and quickly herded his family into the relative safety of the streets. Neighbors gathered in clumps here and there, debating whether the sudden quiet means the end if it or if there will be larger quakes. But it is soon apparent that the earthquake is enough to chase them from their houses, but is not strong enough to cause any real damage in the city.

Ships coming into port, though, soon bring the news of tragedy: Palermo's small scare had been the dying tremors of a great earthquake that had shaken the northeast coast of the island into ruin. Most of Messina and Reggio, two of Sicily's noble cities, were rubble and perhaps 20,000 people were dead. Across the strait, on the mainland, parts of the land in Calabria have been thrown up and others have dropped down. Over the next few days, the tremors come again and again. It is told that in Messina men and buildings buried in the early shocks were sometimes thrown up again in the later ones. Boats full of volunteers wanting to help and others full of opportunists seeking to make a profit if one was to be had rushed to the Messina and to Calabria.

It was soon clear that the earthquake had also shaken Mt. Etna into wakefulness. A few days after the earthquake, Mt. Etna erupted spectacularly. There were many days in which the smoke column rising from the volcano could easily be seen from Palermo, despite the mountains between the two locations.

Old people in the streets spoke of omens and portents of dangers to come. But like most young men, he paid little heed. There were dangers enough in the here and now, without scanning the horizon for future possibilities. Besides there was a new son in his house and a son made a man dream of a very different kind of portents for the future.

Twilight is just beginning as he walks out of the Porta Felice onto the Marina. He catches himself smiling and breathing a little more deeply. He is a little amused that the Marina still affects him so after nearly a lifetime of years. But he simply shrugs and accepts it, like so many citizens of Palermo, he simply loves this place. He loves the long park that runs across the face of Palermo, between the city walls and the sea. He loves the walkways, the beautiful plantings, and the views of the sea, but above all, he loves the Marina's eastern end where it terminates in large terrace and a public garden.

The pathways through the gardens are shaded by large orange and lemon trees and the occasional fir or cypress. Fountains here and there float with aquatic plants and overhead, canaries live and sing in spacious aviaries. He had heard an English painter visiting Palermo call the Marina "the finest feature of Palermo" and describes it as the "great boast and pride of the Palermitans, and it must be confessed that it is the most beautiful promenade in Europe."

Briefly looking about, he crosses the carriage path, not pausing until he is on the walkway that borders the sea. Like many people of Palermo, he comes to the Marina year round, when the weather is good. But he comes most often at twilight in the summers when the cooling sea breezes offer relief from the City's heat.

The local nobility and well-to-do dress in finery and ride their carriages more or less continuously back and forth along the upper marina, nodding to the passengers of other carriages as they pass and stopping occasionally for brief chats. They come here to see and be seen and to socialize with their peers.

As he watches them pass back and forth, he smiles at the ostentation of the expensive carriages and clothing. He knows that many of them have inherited minor titles but little or no wealth. They rent out the best part of their houses and live in small lesser apartments just so that they can afford these fine carriages to keep up appearances.

He prefers it here on the pathways where the common citizens of Palermo, on foot and lacking carriages, can often be seen circled around a story-teller at the marble benches. And best of all, is the Greek styled theater near the center of the Marina where carriages can pull up in a semicircle on one side, while benches are provided on the other side for pedestrians. On warm summer nights, people gather here to enjoy the cool sea air and music from a band that plays from dark until midnight and often later.

The constant ship traffic in the harbor insures that news from all around the Mediterranean comes quickly to Palermo. For most of a year now, Palermo has been hearing news of the French invasion of Northern Italy - led by the Corsican, Napoleone di Buonaparte.

Recently, the rumors were that Napoleone was in Egypt and King Ferdinand was using his absence to strike back at the French. The King did not fare well in battle, and now the French Army was moving south and King Ferdinand IV had suddenly decided that it was time to visit Palermo for an extended stay. The English, who were always happy to discomfit the French, were helping Ferdinand. Indeed, the famous Lord Admiral Nelson of the English Navy was providing the King ferry service from Naples to Palermo.

The boys and young men, his own son included, were excited at all the changes that were going on. Even he could admit to himself that he would probably have been excited at that age. Not anymore; now he understood that the King would be bringing Neapolitan and English soldiers with him. And many idle soldiers, especially foreign soldiers, in Palermo presented too many chances for bad things to happen.

CHAPTER FOUR: WITTLE FAMILY

Mer sott em sei Eegne net verlosse; Gott verlosst die Seine nicht.
(One should not abandon one's own; God does not abandon his own)
- Pennsylvania Dutch saying

Our Wittle and Acri families were located in the Germany, United Kingdom, Italy and Pennsylvania. We are indebted to their struggles and pain, and the ultimate triumph to bring us freedom and opportunity.

Generation Two

The Wittle & Acri parent are including in the second generation, comprising those born in from about 1930 to 1950. Those living are not included in this book, so we move on to the third generation, which would be the grandparents.

Tutte le strade conducono a Roma.

(All roads lead to Rome)

Generation Three

The four grandparents Mildred and Albert Wittle and Sylvia and Amel Acri comprise the Third Generation and is the starting point for the detailed biographies included in this volume.

They are not dead who live in lives they leave behind;
In those whom they have blessed, they live a life again,
And shall live, through the years,
Eternal life, and grow each day more beautiful
As time declares their good,
Forgets the rest, and prove.
                    -    Hugh R. Orr

Albert Elmer Wittle & Mildred Irene Stewart

Albert Elmer Wittle was born on August 14, 1904 in Harrisburg, Pennsylvania. He was one of eight children born to John and Mary Wittle. Albert was more than likely born at home as this was the common birthing practice in 1904. At the time of Albert's birth tuberculous, typhoid and Spanish influenza were in the epidemic stages in Harrisburg. Control of these diseases was hampered by the lack of a proper sanitation system in the city. Raw sewage ran down many of the unpaved streets, thereby polluting the Susquehanna River.

There was a need for major changes in the city. Several of Harrisburg's residents became involved in the City Beautiful Movement to improve the quality of life for Harrisburg residents. The first phase of the City Beautiful was completed when Albert was about eleven years old. Harrisburg transformed from an industrial city covered in mud and filth to a beautiful city with paved streets, a modern sanitary system, clean water, city hall and a covered sewer interceptor along the river. The Harrisburg park system was enlarged by creating Riverfront Park, Reservoir Park, Wildwood Park and the Italian Lake. Albert and his siblings probably played and picnicked in one or all of these parks after their completion.

Around this same time the first wave of what is historically called the Great Migration started. African-Americans from southern states migrated to Harrisburg and the surrounding areas in search of employment. The First World War had just begun and many of the steel and factory workers had gone off to fight. This was the perfect opportunity for many African-Americans and poor whites to move from the economically oppressed South to the North where they could get jobs in the Harrisburg railroad industry and steel mills.

In one year the African-American population of Philadelphia and surrounding cities more than doubled; from approximately 62,000 in 1914 to over 134,000 in 1915. For most of the immigrants, life was harder than they were led to believe by the employment recruiters and black newspapers. They were excluded from most of the labor unions, given the lowest paying and most dangerous jobs. They had to compete with European migrants for housing in overcrowded rundown shanty housing. All of this led to racial unrest, which resulted in a race riot in nearby Chester where three blacks and two whites were killed. This happened when Albert was 13 and then another riot in Philadelphia just a year later.

Oh, the things Albert must have seen and heard about at such a young age. By the time Albert was sixteen years old he had seen many things; the beginning and end of the First World War. The Philadelphia Athletics, forerunners of the Oakland A's, won the World Series in 1910, 1911 and 1913. Chocolate candy mogul, Milton Hershey founded a school for orphaned boys in Hershey, PA. The first black YMCA was established in 1919. He saw the takeover of Pennsylvania Steel by the Bethlehem Steel Company in nearby Steelton and the construction of the Penn-Harris Hotel.

Motel T automobiles were now in mass production, making them more affordable to the middle-class. Perhaps Albert's family was one of the first in his neighborhood to purchase an automobile. His father worked as a locomotive engineer for the Pennsylvania Railroad, surely one of the better paying jobs in the area. The first drive-in gas station, in the country, was built by Gulf Refining Co. in Pittsburg in 1913.

Before the gas station, pumps were located curbside of local businesses such as grocery stores and hardware stores. At these locations multiple cars lining up to refuel caused traffic congestion. In addition to the historical events Albert saw, he also witnessed the birth of his younger sisters, Mary born in 1908 and Leona born in 1913; and the birth of his younger brother, George born in 1911. Albert had four older siblings, Stella, Ross, Alvin and Irvin.

Come the 1920's most homes in Harrisburg had electricity. The popular, at home, entertainment was the radio. When Albert was 18 the first radio station licensed in Harrisburg was WBAK. It was run by the Pennsylvania State Police. Other stations followed; WABB in 1923, WHBG in early 1925 and WPRC started broadcasting in October, 1925. WPRC later changed its call letters to WKBO. As of

2010 it was still operating and owned by Open Heart Ministries, broadcasting Christian contemporary music. Most of the first radio programs were religious services. During the 1920's and even through the 1940's WKBO was broadcast from the Penn-Harris Hotel. The antenna tower was located on the roof of the hotel. The radio often broadcast live events in the hotel ballroom featuring local bands.

The first radio broadcast was made by Pittsburgh station KDKA on Nov.2, 1920. It was Election Day and radio's first announcer, Leo Rosenberg, sent the news that Warren Harding had won the election over James Cox to about 1,000 listeners. The first baseball game to be broadcast was in 1921 by the same radio station. Albert and his family probably spent many hours around the radio listening to Graham McNamee announce every World Series game between 1923 and 1934.

When Albert turned 21, Gene Tunney defeated Jack Dempsey for the World Heavyweight Boxing championship in Philadelphia. No doubt he, his brothers and father listened to the fight on the radio or maybe they drove the Model T to Philadelphia to watch the fight in person. City Beautiful projects were moving forward at this time also. The expansion of the Market Street Bridge from two to four lanes made commuting over the Susquehanna River a lot easier. The construction of the new Capital Complex and its entrance, the State Street Bridge, began when Albert was 21.

Sadly, his father, John, passed away the next year, on May 12, 1927. He was buried in the East Harrisburg Cemetery. Albert may have moved into his parent's home to take care of his mother, as he was still single at this time. A 1930 census registered him at a residence on Susquehanna St. in Harrisburg; the same given for his father at the time of his death.

A few years later the global economic downturn of the Great Depression started with the collapse of Wall Street on Oct. 29, 1929. Most of the world experienced the downturn with unemployment at 25% in the U.S. and up to 33% unemployment in other countries. Albert's mother, Mary, passed away, March 17, 1934, before the major effects of the depression hit the Harrisburg area.

The worst conditions could be felt in single industry towns. Harrisburg however had a greater distribution of political and financial leadership that allowed them to consider a wide range of strategies to weather the storm. Even so, the city did not have enough resources to keep businesses open and residents employed through the end of the depression in 1939/1940.

Beginning in late 1935 the federal work relief program Works Progress Administration (WPA) began employing men to work on various Pennsylvania road projects. At the peak of the program in November of 1938, it employed 143,000 men. This may be where

Albert began his career as a truck driver. He later worked for the City Highway Department as a truck driver.

Mildred Irene Stewart was born on Oct. 21, 1920 in Harrisburg, PA. She was one of seven children born to Johnny and Kathleen Annie Stewart. When she was about 10, the family moved to Wormleysburg, Johnny's hometown. Mildred and Albert were married on Feb. 16, 1943 in Enola, Cumberland County, PA. She was 22 and Albert was 38.

There are a few possibilities as to how Mildred and Albert met. One possibility is that Albert met her when he was working on roads in Cumberland County, PA with the WPA. Or maybe Mildred also worked for the WPA and they met at work. A third possibility could be that the Wittle and Stewart families were already acquainted. Johnny was an auto mechanic working at various garages around the area. Perhaps he worked on John's prized Model T or other automobiles and they struck up a friendship and introduced their children. Regardless of how they met, they fell madly in love and were married in Enola.

They had seven children. All but one child, David, are still living. David passed away in 1970 at the age of 15. Albert passed away on Dec. 25, 1970, when he was 66 years old. He was buried in the East Harrisburg Cemetery. After Albert's death, Mildred remarried. She passed away on Feb. 8, 1985 at the Sunbury Hospital from cardiac arrest due to a blood clot in the heart. She was 64 years old. She was buried in the East Harrisburg Cemetery; we assume next to Albert. At the time of her death she was retired from the PA Department of Transportation. Albert and Mildred's son John carries on the family lineage.

Amel Angelo Acri & Sylvia Frances Barbush

Amel Angelo (Emilio Angiolo) Acri was baptized on July 9, 1904 in J.C. Thompson, Sacred Heart of Jesus, Harrisburg, Dauphin County, Pennsylvania. He was counted in the census in 1910 in Harrisburg, Dauphin County, Pennsylvania. He was educated at School in 1910. He was employed as a Bricklayer helper at local Steel Company in 1920. He was counted in the census in 1920 in Harrisburg, Dauphin County, Pennsylvania. He was counted in the census in 1930. He lived in 7131 Somerset Rd., Harrisburg, Dauphin County, Pennsylvania in 1963.

Amel was affiliated with the St. Catherine Laboure Catholic Church religion in 1963. His funeral took place in 1963 in Daily Funeral, 650 S. 28th St., Harrisburg, Dauphin County, Pennsylvania. He was buried on March 1, 1963 in Holy Cross Cemetery, Harrisburg, Dauphin County, Pennsylvania. He was employed as a Maintenance Supervisor in Dauphin County in 1992. His cause of death was Pulmonary embolism w/acute pancreatitis and post-operative cholodocholithisis. Member: in Holy Name Society, St. Michaels Lodge & Sons of Italy He had a medical condition of cardiac arrest due to blood clot in lung, gall stones, pancreatitis. He was employed as a Steelworker for the local Steel Company. He was employed as a Grocer.

Sylvia Frances (Silvia Francesca) Barbush lived in Via Nanca, Castiglione, Cosenza, Italy in 1908. She immigrated in 1928. She was counted in the census in 1930 in Harrisburg, Dauphin County, Pennsylvania. Her estate was probated in 1992 in Dauphin County, Pennsylvania. She lived in 375 Claremont Dr., Carlisle, Pennsylvania17013 in 1992.

Sylvia was affiliated with the St. Catherine Laboure Catholic Church religion in 1992. She was employed as a Homemaker in 1992. Her funeral took place in 1992 in Neill Funeral Home, 3501 Derry St., Harrisburg, Dauphin County, Pennsylvania. She was buried on March 4, 1992 in Holy Cross Cemetery, Harrisburg, Dauphin County, Pennsylvania. She had a medical condition of pneumonia, cataracts, glaucoma, stroke, hypertension. Her cause of death was Pneumonia. Sylvia was named for her father, "Francesco" Acri. Sylvia and Amel had the following children: Charles Acri, Frank Acri, Teresa F Acri, and Mary Frances Acri.

The following historical tidbits give a sense of this era of our ancestors. The Ford Model T of 1908 was the first automobile mass produced on assembly lines with completely interchangeable parts. It was the automobile that opened up travel to the common middle-class. The innovation of the assembly line was revolutionary.

World War I, beginning in 1914, was a conflict involving most of the world's powers. The beginning of the war was sparked by the assassination of Archduke Franz Ferdinand of Austria Hungary. The world quickly formed into alliances, The Allied Powers—United Kingdom, France, The Russian Empire, and later the United States—fought against the Central Powers—The German Empire, The Austro-Hungarian Empire, The Ottoman Empire and the Kingdom of Bulgaria. Over 70 million military personnel fought in the war including 60 million Europeans. The Western Front consisted of a trench line that changed little until 1917. More than 15 million people were killed; making World War I one of the deadliest conflicts in history.

The Great Depression was a worldwide economic downturn that started with the stock market crash of 1929. The depression varied in countries around the world but generally started in 1929 and lasted until the beginning of World War II. Unemployment rose to 25% in the US and as high as 33% in other countries. Countries whose jobs primarily came from industry suffered the most. The Great Depression was the largest economic downturn in history.

The Holocaust refers to the systematic genocide of over six million European Jews by Nazi Germany. The genocide began in stages in the early 1930's by removing Jews from society; moving the Jews to concentration camps, where they died of slave labor and disease; moving Jews to ghettos; mass shootings in conquered territories; and finally extermination camps where most Jews who survived the journey were killed in gas chambers.

World War II began on September 1, 1939 with the German invasion of Poland. The war involved most of the world's powers and was divided into two sides: the Allies versus the Axis. World War II changed the boundaries of war with significant actions against civilians including the Holocaust and the only use of nuclear weapons in war. 100 million military personnel were involved in the conflict. World War II was the deadliest war in history with over 70 million casualties. World War II ended in 1945 with the victory of The Allies.

Generation Four

Our Fourth Generation includes John and Mary Wittle, John and Catherine Stewart, Frank and Theresa Acri and Raymond and Assunta Barbush of the late 1880's in Pennsylvania and Italy.

Good friend, in the path I have come,
There followed after me to-day
A youth whose feet must pass this way.
This chasm that has been as naught to me
To that fair-haired youth may a pitfall be;
He, too, must cross in the twilight dim;
Good friend, I am building this bridge for him!
- Will A. Dromgoole

GENERATION FOUR

Give me your tired, your poor,
Your huddled masses yearning to breathe free,
The wretched refuse of your teeming shore.
Send these, the homeless, tempest-tossed, to me:
I lift my lamp beside the golden door.
- Emma Lazarus

Our Fourth Generation includes John Elmer Wittle & Mary Elizabeth Minnich, John Stewart & Catherine A Shover, Frank Acri & Theresa Curcio and Raymond Frank Barbush & Maria Assunta DeStephano of the mid to late 1800s. To place them in understandable location and time, the following information was downloaded from our ancestry.com FTM file.

This brief biographical information, and the historical text that follows, will allow the reader to not only identify the starting point of the following biographies, but also allow a better understanding of the times, places and events.

John Elmer Wittle & Mary Elizabeth Minnich

John Elmer Wittle was counted in the census in 1870 in Lower Paxton, Dauphin County, Pennsylvania. He was educated at School between 1870-1880. He was counted in the census in 1880 in Lancaster, Lancaster County, Pennsylvania, living with Annie Killian. He lived in 122 Strawberry Avenue, Harrisburg, Dauphin County, Pennsylvania between 1882-1900. He was employed as a Hostler between 1887-1900. He lived in 117 Broad, Harrisburg, Dauphin County, Pennsylvania between 1887-1900. He lived in 1336 Penn, Harrisburg, Dauphin County, Pennsylvania between 1887-1900.

John was employed as a Fireman between 1887-1900. He was employed as a Fireman in 1893. He lived in 127 Verbeke St., Harrisburg, Dauphin County, Pennsylvania in 1900. He was counted in the census in 1900 in Harrisburg, Dauphin County, Pennsylvania. He was employed as a RR Fireman in 1900. He was counted in the census in 1910 in Susquehanna, Dauphin County, Pennsylvania. He was employed as a Locomotive Engineer in 1910. He lived in 2610 Verbeke St., Harrisburg, Dauphin County, Pennsylvania in 1910. He lived in 1622 Wallace St., Harrisburg, Dauphin County, Pennsylvania in 1920. He was employed as Railroad an Engineer in 1920. He was counted in the census in 1920 in Harrisburg, Dauphin County, Pennsylvania. He was employed as an Engineer for the Pennsylvania

Railroad in 1927. His funeral took place in 1927 in Hawkins Funeral, 1207 N. 3rd St., Harrisburg, Dauphin County, Pennsylvania. He was buried on May 16, 1927 in East Harrisburg Cemetery, Harrisburg, Dauphin County, Pennsylvania. His cause of death was Acute myocarditis. John was named for his grandfather "John" Wittle.

Mary Elizabeth Minnich was counted in the census in 1880 in Harrisburg, Dauphin County, Pennsylvania. She was educated at school in 1880. She lived in Harrisburg, Dauphin County, Pennsylvania in 1893. She was counted in the census in 1900 in Harrisburg, Dauphin County, Pennsylvania. She was counted in the census in 1910 in Susquehanna, Dauphin County, Pennsylvania. She was counted in the census in 1920 in Harrisburg, Dauphin County, Pennsylvania. She lived in Harrisburg, Dauphin County, Pennsylvania in 1930. She lived in H1418 Susquehanna St., Harrisburg, Dauphin County, Pennsylvania in 1930. She was counted in the census in 1930 in Harrisburg, Dauphin County, Pennsylvania.

Mary lived in 1427 Susquehanna St., Harrisburg, Dauphin County, Pennsylvania in 1934. Her funeral took place in 1934 in Harry Pierce, North Third, Harrisburg, Dauphin County, Pennsylvania. She was employed as a Home in 1934. She was buried on March 20, 1934 in East Harrisburg Cemetery, Harrisburg, Dauphin County, Pennsylvania. Her cause of death was Acute cardiac dilatation w/chronic myocarditis with decompensation. Mary Elizabeth was named for her grandmother "Mary Elizabeth" McKim. Mary and John had the following children: Stella Wittle, Ross Henry Wittle, Alvin John Wittle, Irvin H Wittle, Albert Elmer Wittle, Elizabeth "Mary" Wittle, George Wittle and Leona C Wittle.

John Stewart & Catherine A Shover

John "Johnny" Martin Louis Stewart lived in 2nd Street, Wormleysburg, Cumberland, Pennsylvania in 1898. He was counted in the census in 1900 in East Pennsboro, Cumberland County, Pennsylvania. He was counted in the census in 1910 in East Pennsboro, Cumberland County, Pennsylvania. He was educated at School in 1910. He lived in 1222 N Front St., Harrisburg, Dauphin County, Pennsylvania in 1918. He was employed as a Steamboat Engineer for the Hbg Light Heat & Power in 1918. He was counted in the census in 1920.

Johnny lived in 528 North 3rd St., Wormleysburg, Cumberland County, Pennsylvania in 1930. He lived in Wormleysburg, Cumberland County, Pennsylvania in 1930. He was employed as a Mechanic at Kimmels Garage in 1930. He was counted in the census in 1930 in Wormleysburg, Cumberland County, Pennsylvania. He was employed as a Mechanic at an Auto shop in 1930. He was employed as a Mechanic at Philip Bloom in 1936. He lived in 1618 1/2 Fulton, Harrisburg, Dauphin County, Pennsylvania in 1936. He lived in 30 St. extension, Penbrook, Pennsylvania in 1950. He had a medical condition of Height Med, Build Medium, Eyes Gray, Hair D. Brown. His cause of death was Cardiac arrest.

Catherine Ann "Kathleen Annie" Shover was educated at School in 1910. She was counted in the census in 1910 in Harrisburg, Dauphin County, Pennsylvania. She was counted in the census in 1920. She was counted in the census in 1930 in Wormleysburg, Cumberland County, Pennsylvania. She lived in 1225 N. Front St., Harrisburg, Dauphin County, Pennsylvania in 1937.

Catherine was affiliated with the Harrisburg, Dauphin County, Pennsylvania religion in 1965. She lived in Beaufort Farm, Camp Curtain, Estherton, Fort Hunter, Harrisburg, Heckton, Lucknow, Rockville, Uptown, Windsor Farm, all Dauphin County, Pennsylvania in 1981. She lived in 2340 Logan St., Harrisburg, Dauphin County, Pennsylvania17110 in 1981. She lived in Dauphin County, Pennsylvania in 1981. She was employed as a Pennsylvania State Clerk in 1981. Her funeral took place in 1981 in John E Neuemeyer, 1334 N. 2nd St., Harrisburg, Dauphin County, Pennsylvania. She was buried on October 27, 1981 in East Harrisburg Cemetery, Harrisburg, Dauphin County, Pennsylvania. She was adopted in Believed adopted. Her cause of death was Congestive heart failure w/myocardial infarction. It seems probable that Catherine's biological mother was Bessie Shannon and her adoptive mother was Mary Potteiger. Catherine and John had the following children: Mildred Irene Stewart, Robert L Stewart, Doris Stewart, James L Stewart, John C Stewart, Audrey M Stewart and Sarah "Sadie" M Stewart.

Frank Acri & Theresa Curcio

Frank (Francesco) Acri immigrated to Italy to New York, NY in April 1884. He lived in New York, NY about 1890. He was ordained in 1891 in Laborer. He lived in Etna, Allegheny County, Pennsylvania in 1891. Frank may have immigrated more than once to the United States: He immigrated to Italy to New York, NY on the ship Rugia, possibly as a stowaway on March 26, 1894. He immigrated to Italy to New York, NY in 1896. He immigrated to Italy to New York, NY on the ship Ems on February 23, 1899. He immigrated to Italy to New York, NY o the ship Aller on August 8, 1899.

Frank was employed as a Boarder, Unemployed in 1900. He was counted in the census in 1900 in 1st Ward Steelton, Dauphin County, Pennsylvania. He lived in Steelton, Dauphin County, Pennsylvania in 1902. He was employed as a Steelworker in Steelton in 1902. He was naturalized on October 8, 1902 in Pennsylvania. He was employed as a Laborer at the Central Iron and Steel about 1905. He lived in 113 Dock St., Harrisburg, Dauphin County, Pennsylvania in 1909. His funeral took place in 1909 by Speere, 130 South Second Street, Harrisburg, Dauphin County, Pennsylvania. He was employed as a Grocer in 1909. He was buried on March 9, 1909 in Mt. Calvary, Harrisburg, Dauphin County, Pennsylvania. His estate was probated on October 10, 1911 in Dauphin County, Pennsylvania. His cause of death was Cancer liver, exhaustion w/hepatitis. He was affiliated with the St. Mary's, Sharpsburg, Allegheny County, Pennsylvania religion. Frank Acri may have immigrated as stowaway more than once. There may have been two Frank Acris of same age in Steelton, PA. Although Frank died in 1909, he is in 1910 census and has a passport application in 1913.

Theresa (Teresa) Curcio lived in Etna, Allegheny County, Pennsylvania in 1891. She immigrated on June 5, 1893, Italy to New York, NY on the ship Charles Martel. She was employed as a Farmer in 1901. She immigrated on June 13, 1901, Italy to New York, NY on the ship Isola Di Levanzo. She was employed as a Merchant, Owner of Groceries in 1910. She was counted in the census in 1910 in Harrisburg, Dauphin County, Pennsylvania.

Theresa lived in 113 Dock St., Harrisburg, Dauphin County, Pennsylvania in June 1916. She lived in 221 Schuylkill St., Harrisburg, Dauphin County, Pennsylvania in 1920. She was counted in the census in 1920 in Harrisburg, Dauphin County, Pennsylvania. She was employed as a Grocer between 1920-1930. She lived in 2547 N 4th, Harrisburg, Dauphin County, Pennsylvania in 1930. She was counted in the census in 1930 in Pittsburgh, Allegheny County, Pennsylvania. She lived in 113 Dock, Harrisburg, Pennsylvania between 1936-1942. She was employed as a Grocer between 1939-1946. She signed her will in 1950 in Harrisburg, Dauphin County,

Pennsylvania. She was employed as a Housewife in 1951. She lived in 1937 N. 3rd St., Harrisburg, Dauphin County, Pennsylvania in 1951. She was affiliated with the Our Lady of the Blessed Sacrament, Harrisburg, Dauphin, Pennsylvania religion in 1951. Her funeral took place in 1951 in Jos. A. Wiedeman Funeral Home, 357 South Third Street, Steelton, Dauphin County, Pennsylvania. She was buried on October 31, 1951 in Mt. Calvary, Harrisburg, Dauphin County, Pennsylvania. Her estate was probated on November 13, 1951 in Harrisburg, Dauphin County, Pennsylvania. Her cause of death was Myocardial infarction w/ coronary occlusion and coronary artery disease. Theresa and Frank had the following children: Charles H Acri, Mary Angelina Acri, Michael Acri, Sarah "Sadie" Ernestine Acri, James A Acri, Amel Angelo Acri, John Acri, Alfred Acri and Ella G Acri.

Raymond Frank Barbush & Maria Assunta DeStephano

Raymond Frank (Raimondo Francesco) Barbush lived in Via Nanca, Castiglione, Cosenza, Italy in 1880. He immigrated on November 12, 1894. He was counted in the census in 1900 in Hazel, Luzerne County, Pennsylvania. He was naturalized on May 21, 1906 in Wilkes-Barre, Pennsylvania. He was employed as a Farmer in 1908. He lived in Via Nanca, Castiglione, Cosenza, Italy in 1908. He immigrated in 1909, Hamburg to USA. He was counted in the census in 1910 in Hazelton, Luzerne County, Pennsylvania. He served in the WWI military about 1919. He was counted in the census in 1920. He immigrated on January 6, 1921 on the Regina d'Italia.

Raymond was employed as a Barber in 1930. He lived in 910 North 4th, Harrisburg, Dauphin County, Pennsylvania in 1930. He lived in Barbershop, 1016 Market St., Harrisburg, Dauphin County, Pennsylvania in 1930. He was counted in the census in 1930 in Harrisburg, Dauphin County, Pennsylvania. He lived in 910 6th St., Harrisburg, Dauphin County, Pennsylvania between 1930-1942. His funeral took place in 1945 in GH Sourbier, Harrisburg, Dauphin County, Pennsylvania. He lived in 34 N. 19th St., Harrisburg, Dauphin County, Pennsylvania in 1945. He was employed as a Bar owner in 1945. He was buried on September 20, 1945 in Holy Cross Cemetery, Harrisburg, Dauphin County, Pennsylvania. His cause of death was

Coronary occlusion w/hypertension cardiovascular disease. He had a medical condition of Height 5'6", Weight 147, White, Brown eyes, Gray-Black hair, dark complexion, wears glasses and moustache.

Maria "Sadie" Assunta DeStephano was employed as a Homemaker about 1900. She was employed as a Farmer in 1908. She was buried in 1918. Maria was named for her grandmother "Maria" Acri. Maria and Raymond had the following children: Sylvia Frances and Frances Barbush.

CITATIONS

The following are the complete source citations of all genealogies from the TFH compilation, broken down into the four genealogies, Thompson, Curry/Mazo, Romano and Wittle.

THOMPSON SOURCES

1 Gerald G Thompson, Middletown, PA, June, 2010.1 Shirley Mary Duncan, #1487170-1935, 11-29-1935, Snyder Co, PA, Department of Vital Records, New Castle, PA.
2 Gerald Gilbert Thompson birth record, #1170270-1935, 09-23-1935, Dauphin Co, PA, Department of Vital Records, New Castle, PA.
3 Harper Bruce Thompson birth record, #344701, #122649-07, September 1907, Schuylkill Co, PA, Department of Vital Records, New Castle, PA.
4 Harper B Thompson death certificate, #2501265, Department of Vital Records, New Castle, PA.
5 Harper B Thompson, Obituary, Harrisburg Patriot Newspaper, July 1981.
6 Thompson-Batdorf marriage record, Register of Wills, Clerk of Orphans Court, Dauphin Co, PA, 1935.
7 Samuel Peters, Descendants of John Peters, Evelyn S. Hartman.
8 Myrtle A. Batdorf birth certificate, January 1918, Department of Vital records, New Castle, PA.
9 Myrtle Thompson, Obituary, Harrisburg Patriot newspaper, 1983.
10 Myrtle A Thompson death certificate, #3455802, Department of Vital records, New Castle, PA.
11 Duncan family information, Jack Lehman, North Charleston, SC.
12 William Duncan, April 1978, PA, Social Security Death Index, www.familysearch.org.
13 Irvin Francis Duncan, Birth record, Northumberland Co County Courthouse, Register of Wills, Sunbury, PA.
14 Irvin Duncan, April 1978, PA, Social Security Death Index, www.familysearch.org.
15 Irvin Francis Duncan death certificate, #0030831, Northumberland Co, PA, Department of Vital Records, New Castle, PA.
16 Mary Lucetta Anderson, Memoranda, Bob Anderson, PA, rmorris@ptd.net.
17 Mamie Duncan, April 1989, PA, Social Security Death Index, www.familysearch.org.
18 Mamie Lucetta Duncan death certificate, #0078833, #069201, April 1989, Department of Vital Record, New Castle, PA.
19 Mamie Luzetta Anderson, #061660-1908, 04-13-1908, Northumberland Co, PA, Department of Vital Records, New Castle, PA.
20 Mamie L Duncan, Probate file, 47-89-85, microfiche, Montour County Courthouse, Office of the Reg and Recorder, Danville, PA, Norman Nicol, ndnicol@epix.net, Mar 2008.
21 Abel Thompson death certificate, #0506211, #133775-93, January 1918, Department of Vital Records, New castle, PC.
22 Thompson-Hensel Marriage, Office of the Register of Wills, Schuylkill County, PA, June 1904.
23 Abel Robert Thompson, WW I Draft Reg Cards, 1917-1918 Record, www.ancestry.com.
24 Abel R Thompson, Probate file, 1918, unnumbered original papers, 34pp, Schuylkill Co Courthouse, Schuylkill, PA, Norman Nicol, Apr 2008.
25 Gussie May Thompson death certificate, #0506187, #31982, March 1973, Department of Vital Records, New Castle, PA.
26 Gussie May Hensel, Funeral obituary, March 1973.
27 Gussie Mae Thompson, Obituary, Pottsville Repulbican, Pottsville, PA, March 28, 1973.
28 Gussie M. Thompson, Greenwood Cemetery, Tower City, Schuylkill Co, PA, John Barket, Tower City, PA, B-3-1.
29 Gussie M. Thompson, Reg of Will book, Book 145, pp578-82, May 27, 1950, probated Sept 11, 1973, Schuylkill Co Courthouse, Schuylkill, PA, Norman Nicol, Apr 2008.
30 Michael Goodman, Descendants of Michael Goodman, Evelyn S Hartman, deanh@voicenet.com.
31 Abel F Thompson, Bob Averell Family Tree, Entries: 7956, Updated: 2004-08-01 00:29:03 UTC (Sun), Contact: Bob Averell.
32 Lydia Mae Thompson, Obituary, Pottsville Repulbican, Pottsville, PA, Jan 18, 1983.
33 James Edward Batdorf death certificate, #0506183, #66234-39, August 1954, Department of Vital Records, New Castle, PA.
4 James Edward Batdorf, Church record, Rev. O.S. Moyer, Angie Eddy, Maple Grove Cemetery, Eluzabethville, PA, p 29.

35 James Edward Batdorf, United States WW II Draft Reg. Cards, 1942 Record, 2243624, www.ancestry.com.

36 James Edward Batdorf, Social Security numident record, application for SS-5, SSA, Nov 2006, Baltimore, MD.

37 Batdorf-Wert marriage record, Church record, Rev. O.S. Moyer, Angie Eddy, Maple Grove Cemetery, Elizabethville, PA, p 16.

38 Beulah I Batdorf death certificate, #0506188, #057537, June 1983, Department of Vital records, New Castle, PA.

39 Beulah Batdorf, June 1983, PA, Social Security Death Index, www.familysearch.org.

40 Beulah I Batdorf, Obituary, Harrisburg Patriot News, 1983.

41 John Peters, Peters family information, Evelyn S Hartman, deanh@voicenet.com.

42 Peter Batdorf, Descendants of Peter Batdorf, Evelyn S Hartman, deanh@voicenet.com.

43 Duncan-Layman mariage record, #8855, Northumberland Co, PA, 1899, Northumberland Co County Register of Wills.

44 Wm Duncan death certificate, #0030852, #90924, Northumberland Co, PA, Department of Vital records, New Castle, PA.

45 Duncan family information, Stephanie Gormley.

46 Duncan-Layman marriage record, April 20, 1899, Edward C. Eisley.

47 Duncan-Layman marriage record, #8855, Northumberland Co, PA, 1899, Northumberland Co County Register of Wills, Sunbury, PA.

48 Duncan-Layman marriage record, #8855, Northumberland Co, PA, 1899, Northumberland Co County Register of Wills.

49 Lottie V. Willard, death certificate, File #29987, Reg #19, #3505042, February 1936, Department of Vital Records, New Castle, PA.

50 William Duncan, Pomfret Manor Cemetery, Sunbury, Northumberland Co, PA, NCHS, The Hunter House, Sunbury, PA.

51 Duncan household, 1900 United States Census, microfilm image, PA State Library. Died Sunbury, PA, Duncan family information, Stephanie Gormley.

52 Charlotte Layman, Duncan family information, Stephanie Gormley.

53 Anderson-Keefer marriage record, Northumberland Co, PA, Northumberland Co Register of Wills, #11421.

54 William Anderson, May 1969, PA, Social Security Death Index, www.familysearch.org.

55 William Morris Anderson death certificate, #0740733, #050910-69, May 1969, Department of Vital Records, New Castle, PA.

56 William M. Anderson, Cemetery records, Orchard Hills Cemetery and Memorial Park, Shamokin Dam, PA, Janet, Section 3, Lot 188.

57 Anderson-Keefer marriage record, July 15, 1902, Northumberland Co, PA, Northumberland Co Register of Wills, #11421.

58 Bible p, Marriage records, source unknown.

59 Memoranda, Bob Anderson, PA, rmorris@ptd.net.

60 Emma L. Keefer, Bible p, Birth records, source unknown.

61 Emma Louisa Anderson death certificate, #0740677, #53801-503, April 1963, Department of Vital Records, New Castle, PA.

62 Emma Louisa Keefer, Northumberland Co, PA, 1861-92, Zion Evangelical Lutheran Church, search.ancesry.com.

63 Emma Louisa Anderson death certificate, #0740677, #53801-503, April 1963, Department of Vital Records, New Castle, PA.

64 Emma L. Anderson, Cemetery records, Orchard Hills Cemetery and Memorial Park, Shamokin Dam, PA, Janet, Section 3, Lot 188.

65 William Morris Anderson, #0740733, #050910-69, May 1969, Department of Vital Records, New Castle, PA.

66 William Maurice Anderson, U.S. World War 1 Draft Registration Cards, No 1674, 3-27-0, Snyder, PA, 1917, www.ancestry.com.

67 Emma L. Anderson, Emma Louise Anderson, obituary, Sunbury newspaper.

68 Robert B Thompson death certificate, #0042512, #102079, Reg # 102, October 1907, Department of Vital records, New Castle, PA.

69 Robert B Thompson, Greenwood Cemetery, Tower City, Schuylkill Co, PA, John Barket, Tower City, PA, B-1-1.

70 Thompson family information, John L linden, jllinden@comcast.net.

71 Alexander Thompson, Schuylkill County, PA, p 1054.

72 Lydia B. Thompson, Greenwood Cemetery, Tower City, Schuylkill Co, PA, John Barket, Tower City, PA, B-1-1.

73 Bob Averell Family Tree, Bob Averell, raverell@carolina.rr.com, awt.ancestry.com.

74 Howard A.C. Hensel, #0036895, #63360, Reg # 66, June 1927, Department of Vital records, New Castle, PA.

75 Hensel family information, Victor Hensel, NJ.

76 Howard Andrew Carson Hensel, Howard Andrew Carson Hensel probate file, 1927, unnumbered orginal papers, 21pp, probated June 29, 1927, Schuylkill Co Courthouse, Schuylkill, PA, Norman Nicol, Apr 2008.

77 Clara M Hensel death certificate, #0042528, #37124, Reg # 29, March 1926, Department of Vital records, New Castle, PA.

78 Casper Hansel, Descendants of Casper (LaHentzelle) Hensel, Evelyn S Hartman, deanh@voicenet.com.

79 Batdorf Family information, Virginia Faust.

80 Thomas Batdorf, #0102590, #81400-17, 1916, Department of Vital records, New Castle, PA.

81 Mary L Batdorf, #0042526, #7?-23, 1924, Department of Vital records, New Castle, PA.

82 John Wert, #0042527, #95868-1303, 1924, Department of Vital records, New Castle, PA.

83 Adeline Row, St. John Evangelical Lutheran Church, Berrysburg, PA, Sara S. Neagley, Elizabethville, PA. 84 Mrs. Adeline Wert death certificate, #26162, #3457526, March 1921, Department of Vital Records, New Castle, PA.

85 Descendants of Frederick Adam Faber, Evelyn S Hartman, deanh@voicenet.com.

86 Johann Heinrich Friedrich Dankert, Ancestry.com. Germany, Select Births and Baptisms, 1558-1898 [database on-line]. Deutschland, Geburten und Taufen 1558-1898 Germany, Select Births and Baptisms, 1558-1898, Provo, UT, USA: Ancestry.com Operations, Inc., 2014. Original data: Germany, Births and Baptisms, 1558-1898. Salt Lake City, Utah: FamilySearch, 2013.

87 Catherine Duncan, Death certificate, Northumberland Co County Register of Wills, Sunbury, PA.

88 Duncan family information, Stephanie Gormley, PA, 1989.

89 Melinda Duncan, Cemetery record, Apr 1933, A genealogists Guide to Burials in Northumberland Co, PA, Vol I, Meiser & Meiser, 1989.

90 Sallie Duncan, Cemetery record, Apr 1933, A genealogists Guide to Burials in Northumberland Co, PA, Vol I, Meiser & Meiser, 1989.

91 Sarah Duncan, Baptisms of Infants, Zion Evan Luth Register, 1851-1892, Sunbury, PA, p41.

92 Hannah Artilla Duncan, Baptisms of Infants, Zion Evan Luth Register, 1851-1892, Sunbury, PA, p94.

93 Charley Duncan, Baptisms of Infants, Zion Evan Luth Register, 1851-1892, Sunbury, PA, p101.

94 Layman/Lehman family information, Files, NCHS, The Hunter House, Sunbury, PA.

95 Joseph Pierce Layman, death record, Illinois Statewide Death Index, 1916-1950, www.cyberdriveillinois.com/GenealogyMWeb/ODPHdeathsearch.

96 Joseph Pierce Layman, State of IL, Dept of Public Health, DVS, Reg #4976, Primary Dt #3104, Cook, IL, Feb 1924.

97 Lehman-Oberlander marriage, source unknown.

98 Rebecca Lehman (Layman) death certificate, #105066, Reg # 456, #3457529, November 1921, Department of Vital Records, New Castle, PA.

99 Lucetta Anderson death certificate, #0740660, #117712-223, November 1916, Department of Vital records, New Castle, PA.

100 Anderson family information, Stephanie Gormley, PA.

101 Bible p, Birth records, source unknown.

102 James P Keefer death record abstract, August 4, 1892, Edward C. Eisley.

103 Thompson family information, Jim Thompson, jbthompson@compuserve.com, pp 4-11.

104 Thompson family information, Films from 1993, Jane L Fouraker, Lancaster Co, PA.

105 Thompson family information, Jim Thompson, jbthompson@compuserve.com, pp 4-11 & Thompson family information, Irene C. Stearns, DeKalb, IL.

106 Isabel Penman, Vital records Index, British Isles, Intellectual Reserve Inc, 8/5/2010.

107 Thompson family information, Irene C. Stearns, DeKalb, IL.

108 Alexander Thompson, Schuylkill County, PA, p 668-669.

109 Alexander Thompson, Miners Journal, December 5, 1873.

110 Mrs. Thompson, Burial record, Miners Journal deaths, 1851.

111 Michael Goodman, Tower City, Porter Centennial, 1868-1968, p 188.

112 Michael Goodman, Obituatary, FROM 'THE WEST SCHUYLKILL HERALD', 03 JANUARY 1901, Jeffrey A. Brown, ntrprz@dmv.com.

113 Michael Gurtmann, "Pennsylvania, Births and Christenings, 1709-1950," index, FamilySearch (https://familysearch.org/pal:/MM9.1.1/V2NX-KXS : accessed 19 Nov 2014), Michael Gutmann, 12 May 1811; Christening, citing SAINT JOHNS LUTHERAN CHURCH NEAR BERRYSBURG,MIFFLIN TWP,DAUPHIN,PENNSYLVANIA; FHL microfilm 845111.

114 Michael Goodman death certificate, #1252, May 1901, Dauphin County Register of Wills, Harrisburg, PA.

115 Hensel-Workman marriage record, 1853, Register of Wills, Dauphin Co, PA.

116 Hensel family information, Dauphin Co Marriages, 1852-1855, CAGS.

117 Hensel family information, History of Michael Hensel (Hentzel) Sr. & His Related Families, R. Longtin-Thompson.

118 Andrew Gise Hensel death certificate, #0036891, #115081, Reg # 84, December 1908, Department of Vital records, New Castle, PA.

119 Andrew Gise Hensel, #0036891, #115081, Reg # 84, December 1908, Department of Vital records, New Castle, PA.

120 Daniel Updegrove death certificate, #1071, March 1899, Dauphin County Register of Wills, Harrisburg, PA.

121 Updegrove Family information, Updegrove Genealogy, PA State library.

122 Daniel Updegrove, Vital records, Dauphin County, p 26.

123 Mrs. Sarah Updegrove death certificate, #0042525, #81494, File 42, Reg 2193, July 1923, Department of Vital Records, New Castle, PA.

124 Welkers in the USA & Nulls from PA, Greg Welker, gwelker@chesapeake.net, awt.ancestry.com.

125 Baddorf Family, Gratz History, p 193.

126 Peter Batdorf, St. Peters (Hoffmans) Union Church, Burials.

127 Peter Botdorf, St. Peter's (Hoffman's) Union Church, Lykens, Dauphin Co, PA, Gert Mysliwski, gert@foothill.net.

128 Peter Batdorf, Hoffmans Reformed Church, Lykens Valley, Dauphin Co, PA, Historical & Genealogical, pp 227-8.

129 Peter Batdorf, Probate files, 1881, Affidavit Rep #5, Dauphin County Courthouse, Reg of Wills, Deborah Hershey, Elizabethtown, PA, Mar 2008.

130 Elizabeth Batdorf, Hoffmans Reformed Church, Lykens Valley, Dauphin Co, PA, Historical & Genealogical, pp 227-8.

131 Mary Peters death certificate, bk C, #945, 1897, Dauphin County Register of Wills, Harrisburg, PA.

132 Mary Peters death certificate, Dauphin County Register of Wills, bk C, #945, 1897, Harrisburg, PA, 140, bk C, #945, 1897, Perry County Historians.

133 Mary Peters death certificate, Dauphin County Register of Wills, bk C, #945, 1897, Harrisburg, PA.

134 Wert Family, Jonathan Wert.

135 David Wert death certificate, Dauphin County Register of Wills, bk E, #852, December 20, 1900, , Harrisburg, PA.

136 Shoop family information, Are you my cousin, Howard Ward, haroldw1@juno.com, awt.ancestry.com.

137 Monn & Related Families, Danni Monn Hopkins, clueless@clnk.com, awt.ancestry.com.

138 David Wert (West) death record, Extract from County Death records, 1893-1906.

139 Wert household, 1870 United States Census, Dauphin Co, PA, PA State library microfilm.

140 Wertz family information, Bob Messerschmidt, Laurel, MD, SusanM4383@aol.com.

141 Wertz family information, Cindi Grimm, Grimm@ruralife.net.

142 Daniel Row, Baptismal record, St. John Evangelical Lutheran Church, Dauphin Co, PA, p 64.

143 Rowe family information, Howard E Row, Dover, DE.

144 Daniel Rowe, St. John Evangelical Lutheran Church, Berrysburg, PA, Sara S. Neagley, Elizabethville, PA, 424 6M 24D.

145 Susanna Rowe, St. John Evangelical Lutheran Church, Berrysburg, PA, Sara S. Neagley, Elizabethville, PA.

146 Joh Heinr Dankert, Mecklenburg-Schwerin Volkszählung, 1819 Mecklenburg-Schwerin, Germany, Ancestry.com. Mecklenburg-Schwerin, Germany, Census, 1819 [database on-line]. Provo, UT, USA: Ancestry.com Operations Inc, 2007. Original data: Mecklenburg-Schwerin (Großherzogtum), Volkszählungsamt. Volkszählung 1819. Landeshauptarchiv Schwerin. 2.21-4/4 Bevölkerungs-, Geburts-,Konfirmations-, Heirats- und Sterbelisten.

147 Gerhard Wilhelm Heinrich Dankert, Deutschland, Geburten und Taufen 1558-1898 Germany, Select Births and Baptisms, 1558-1898 Ancestry.com. Germany, Select Births and Baptisms, 1558-1898 [database on-line]. Provo, UT, USA: Ancestry.com Operations, Inc., 2014. Original data: Germany, Births and Baptisms, 1558-1898. Salt Lake City, Utah: FamilySearch, 2013.

148 Sophia Magaretha Qualmann, Mecklenburg-Schwerin Volkszählung, 1819 Mecklenburg-Schwerin, Germany, Census, 1819 Ancestry.com. Mecklenburg-Schwerin, Germany, Census, 1819 [database on-line]. Provo, UT, USA: Ancestry.com Operations Inc, 2007.

149 Carolina Maria Henriette Kelling, Deutschland, Geburten und Taufen 1558-1898 Germany, Select Births and Baptisms, 1558-1898, Ancestry.com. Germany, Select Births and Baptisms, 1558-1898 [database on-line]. Provo, UT, USA: Ancestry.com Operations, Inc., 2014. Original data: Germany, Births and Baptisms, 1558-1898. Salt Lake City, Utah: FamilySearch, 2013.

150 Caroline Maria Henriette Kelling, Deutschland, Tote und Beerdigungen 1582-1958 Germany, Select Deaths and Burials, 1582-1958 Ancestry.com. Germany, Select Deaths and Burials, 1582-1958 [database on-line]. Provo, UT, USA: Ancestry.com Operations, Inc., 2014. Original data: Germany, Deaths and Burials, 1582-1958. Salt Lake City, Utah: FamilySearch, 2013.

151 David McCord, Family tree. https://familysearch.org/tree/#view=tree&person=935Q-7XG&section=pedigree, familysearch.org.

152 David McCloud, Probate files, 1864, Northumberland County Courthouse, Reg of Wills, Sunbury, Bk 5, p261, PA, Robyn Jackson, genealogylover@msn.com, 2008.

153 Jeremiah McCloud, Pennsylvania, Death Certificates, 1906-1924 forJeremiah McCloud, ancestry.com.

154 McCloud-Frye, Marriage, Northumberland County, SS, #2856, Register & Recorder, Sunbury, PA, Oct 1890, Market St, Sunbury, PA.

155 Michael Layman, Bethel ME Cemetery, p 151, Jerome K. Hively, Brogue, PA.

156 Elmira Layman, Bethel ME Cemetery, p 151, Jerome K. Hively, Brogue, PA.

157 Duncan family information, 1870 United States Census, York Co, PA, Roll M593-1468, p 545, Image 700, ancestry.com & Microfilm, PA State Library, Hbg, PA.

158 Overlander-Kipe marriage record, #662-59, Calender of Vital Records of the Counties of York & Adams.

159 Sarah Oberlander, Probate files, 1874, Rep 42, York County Archives, York, PA, Deborah Hershey, Elizabethtown, PA, Dec 2008.

160 Casper Arnold, Crossley/Gunsallus/Kimmel Family, Worldconnect Project, worldconnect.rootsweb.com.

161 Anderson family information, Jim Anderson, Ontario, CAN.

162 Elijah Anderson, January 1820, Record of Grubb's (Botschaft) Lutheran Church, 1792-1875.

163 Elijah Anderson, Tombstone Incriptions of Snyder County, PA, M.B. Lontz, 1981.

164 Arnold family information, Snyder County pioneers, Snyder County.

165 Family Ties, Laurie Lendosky, llendosky@cyberia.com, awt.ancestry.com/cgi-bin/igm-cgi.

166 Cath. Anderson, 1893, Tombstone Inscriptions of Snyder County, PA, M.B. Lontz, 1981, Union County Historical Society.

167 Catherine Anderson, Letters of Adminstration, 1893, Snyder County Courthouse, Register of Wills.

168 Anderson family information, Stephanie Gormley, PA & Descendants of Philip Jacob Bordner, John Getz, jgetz@iu.net.

169 Croce/Walker Family Tree, Sue Walker, smawalker@comcast.net, awt.ancestry.com.

170 Abraham Gaugler death certificate, August 1900, Snyder County Register of Wills, Middleburg, PA.

171 Abraham Gaugler, Obituary, Middleburg Post, Thu Aug 30, 1900, c/o Pat Smith, pms9848@hotmail.com.

172 Some of my ancestors, David A. Miller, david.miller@nwa.com, awt.ancestry.com.

173 Kelly family information, Sue Dufour, sdufour@skyenet.net.

174 Kesiah Gaugler, Mount Zion United Brethren Church Cemetery, Snyder Co, PA, Shaffer & Arnold, 1904, www.rootsweb.com.

175 Mrs Annie Duttry, Pennsylvania, Death Certificates, Ancestry.com. Pennsylvania, Death Certificates, 1906-1963 [database on-line]. Provo, UT, USA: Ancestry.com Operations, Inc., 2014.

176 Gougler/Thursby family information, Jean Doherty, jmd17601@yahoo.com.

177 Kieffer family information, www.geocities.com/jimmyk418/surname.htm.

178 Family of Eldon G. Keefer, Eldon G. Keefer, PeterKeefer@aol.com, awt.keefer.com.

179 Kieffer family information, Family Group record, Jere S. Keefer, Mercersburg, PA.

180 M.A. Keefer death certificate, February 1904, Northumberland Co County Register of Wills, Sunbury, PA.

181 Michael A. Keefer, Spruce St. Cemetery, Sunbury, Northumberland Co County Historical Society.

182 Keefer, Kiefer file, Northumberland Co County Historical Society, Sunbury, PA, Floyd, p 346.

183 Margaret M Keefer death certificate, April 1899, Northumberland Co County Register of Wills, Sunbury, PA.

184 Margaret M. Keefer, Spruce St. Cemetery, Sunbury, Northumberland Co County Historical Society.

185 Margaret M Keefer death record abstract, April 1899, Edward C. Eisley.

186 Margaret M Keefer death record, May 6, 1899, Northumberland Co County Register of Wills, PA, Sunbury, PA.

187 Margaret M Keefer, Obituary, Sunbury newspaper, Robert C. Eisley.

188 Michael A. Keefer, Spruce St. Cemetery, Sunbury, Northumberland Co County Historical Society.

189 Michael A. Keefer, Keefer, Kiefer files, Northumberland Co County Historical Society, Sunbury, PA.

190 Keefer family information, Family of Eldon G. Keefer, Eldon G. Keefer, PeterKeefer@aol.com, awt.keefer.com.

191 The Livezey Family, Sixth Generation, The Livezey Association, p 152.

192 Anna M Livezly, Death record, 388, Aug 1910, Warren, Massachusetts, Connie Taylor <connieataylor@icloud.com>.

193 Livezty household, 1900 Census, "Livetzly" household, 1900 United States Federal Census, SD 6, ED 147, Sheet 12, Cumberland, NJ, www.ancestry.com & Microfilm, PA State Library, Hbg, PA.

194 Livezty household, 1900 United States Federal Census, SD 6, ED 147, Sheet 12, Cumberland, NJ, www.ancestry.com & Microfilm, PA State Library, Hbg, PA.

195 Robert Thompson, Ancestry Publci trees, O'Brien Family Tree, Owner: christine hillstead, ancestry.com.

196 Thompson family information, Jane Fouraker, mjfour@mindpsring.com.

197 Robert Thompson, Thompson History, Jim Thompson, jbthompson@compuserve.com, pp 4-11, Thompson family information, John B. Linden, Lynden@comcast.net.

198 Penman family information, Jim Thompson, jbthompson@compuserve.com.

199 David Penman, FHL, Pedigree chart, www.ancestry.com.

200 David Penman, Penman family information, John Penman, PenmanJC@aol.com.

201 John Penman, Vital records Index, British Isles, Intellectual Reserve Inc, 8/5/2010.

202 Goodman family data, DESCENDANTS OF GEORGE GOODMAN OF BETHEL TOWNSHIP, BERKS CO, Lawrence Goodman, lawrenceeg@comcast.net, http://www.goodmangenealogy.com/1104.htm.

203 Michael Gudman, Bethel. January 25, 1810. http://berks.pa-roots.com/.

204 Peter Brown, Tyson Family_2012-03-18, Owner: Gary Tyson, ancestry.com.

205 Brown family information, Peter Brown descedants, Deb Kandybowksi, debkandy@epix.net.

206 Andreas Hansel, Baptism, York Co, PA library, cards on file.

207 Andrew Hensel, Christ Church, Littlestown, PA, Adams Co County 18th records lookup, Virginia, vperry1@shawneelink.net.
208 Andrew Hensel, Death of an Old Soldier, Obituary, New Bloomfield newspaper, July 1875.
209 Andrew Hensel, Source 146, index card, Perry County Historians.
210 Mrs. Hensel, Source 140 & 146, index cards, Perry County Historians.
211 Mrs. Mary Hensel, New Bloomfield Times, January 20, 1877.
212 Mary Hensel, U.S., Find A Grave Index, 1600s, Ancestry.com. U.S., Find A Grave Index, 1600s-Current [database on-line]. Provo, UT, USA: Ancestry.com Operations, Inc., 2012. Original data: Find A Grave. Find A Grave. http://www.findagrave.com/cgi-bin/fg.cgi.
213 Workman family information, Evelyn Hartman, Evelyn S Hartman, deanh@voicenet.com.
214 Joseph Workman, Wiconisco Calvary Cemetery, Rhonda, yeahbaby@penn.com, Row 4.
215 Joseph Workman, U.S., Find A Grave Index, 1600s, Ancestry.com. U.S., Find A Grave Index, 1600s-Current [database on-line]. Provo, UT, USA: Ancestry.com Operations, Inc., 2012. Original data: Find A Grave. Find A Grave. http://www.findagrave.com/cgi-bin/fg.cgi.
216 ibid.
217 The Romberger Line, Ancestors of Richard Alan Lebo.
218 Romberger Family, St. John's Lutheran Church, p 10, John Romberger.
219 Johann Uptegrav, 1805, Jacobs Church, Pine Grove, Swedberg, SCUR III, p 240.
220 Updegrove Family information, Rosie Byard, rbyard@bigfoot.com.
221 John Upderove, Smith Family Tree, Owner: hannibal8901, ancestry.com.
222 Rutzel Family Genealogy, David Rutzel, leztur@hotmail.com, awt.ancestry.com.
223 Elizabeth Reiss, Provizzi Family Tree, Owner: sprovizzi, ancestry.com.
224 Kulp family information, J. Wagner, Union County.
225 Mrs Elizabeth Kulp, Pennsylvania and New Jersey, Church and Town Records, 1708-1985 about Mrs Elizabeth Culp. Source Citation: Historical Society of Pennsylvania; Historic Pennsylvania Church and Town Records; Reel: 234.
226 Peter Batdorf, Descendants of Peter Batdorf, Evelyn S. Hartman.
227 Valentine Welker, Direct Descendants of Valentine (Welcher) Welker, Evelyn S. Hartman.
228 Dauphin County Names, Data p, Robert M Howard, www://genealogy.lv/howard/.
229 Welker family information, Roger Cramer, rogercubs@aol.com.
230 John Welker, U.S., Find A Grave Index, 1600s-Current, Ancestry.com. U.S., Find A Grave Index, 1600s-Current [database on-line]. Provo, UT, USA: Ancestry.com Operations, Inc., 012. Original data: Find A Grave. Find A Grave. http://www.findagrave.com/cgi-bin/fg.cgi.
231 Welker Family, Gratz History, p 450-455.
232 Pats Family, Pat Scott, pat.scott@comcast.net, awt.ancestry.com.
233 Elizabeth Messerschmidt, Pennsylvania Church Records - Adams, Berks, and Lancaster Counties, 1729-1881 about Elizabeth Messerschmidt.
234 Peters Research, Michael McCormick, Enduring Legacy, Gardners, PA, Feb 2009.
235 Peters household, 1850 United States Federal Census, Union, PA, 288, ancestry.com & Microfilm, PA State Library, Hbg, PA.
236 Maria Peters, Death notice, Lewisburg Chronicle, Oct. 1852 c/o Union County Historical Society, Maggie Miller, hstorici@ptd.net.
237 Jacob Wert, Wert family, Onetree, ancestry.com.
238 Elizabeth Wert death record, Extract from County Death records, 1893-1906.
239 Shoop family information, Are you my cousin, Harold Ward, haroldw1@juno.com, awt.ancestry.com.
240 Shoop family information, Northumberland Co County, PA 1777-1865, Stone Valley Lutheran, www.ancestry.com.
241 Johannes Schup, Stone Valley Cemetery, Robert Straub, Dalmatia, PA, Section A, Row 16, Grave 30.
242 Wert Family, Jonathan Wert, www.mdi-wert.com.
243 Sarah Wertz, David C Paul, Owner: dcpnascar7781, ancestry.com.
244 The Lunnys, William Lunny, rlunny@msn.com, awt.ancestry.com.
245 Frank Rowe, FHL, Pedigree chart, www.familysearch.org.
246 William Rowe, Family Data Collection, Individual Records, www.ancestry.com, Edmund West, comp.

247 William Rowe, Rowe family, Onetree, ancestry.com.

248 William Rowe, Descendants of Frank (Rau) Rowe, Evelyn S. Hartman.

249 Johann Wilhelm Frantz, Descendants of Johann Wilhelm Frantz, Evelyn S. Hartman.

250 Adam Frantz, Frantz family, Onetree, ancestry.com.

251 Gieseman family information, Mary Smith.

252 Franz-Gieseman marriage record, October 1811, source unknown.

253 Susanna Franz, St. John's Congr., 17 feb 1826, Mifflin, Dauphin Co, PA, Gert, gert@foothill.net.

254 Franz-Gieseman marriage record, October 1811, Lykens Valley lower church (David's Reformed) Millersburg, Upper Paxton, Dauphin Co, 1774-1844.

255 Susanna Franz, St. John's Congr.17 feb 1826, Mifflin, Dauphin Co, PA, Gert Mysliwski, gert@foothill.net.

256 Michael Lyman, David R. Layman, Biography, source unknown.

257 Lehman-Klein marriage record, June 28, 1818, Church Book records 4.

258 Lehman-Klein marriage record, Marriages at Trinity Lutheran Church, Lancaster Co, PA, Joan E. Kahler, Charles.Kahler@worldnet.att.net.

259 David R. Layman, Biography, source unknown.

260 John Rieman, 1850 United States Federal Census, Year: 1850; Census Place: York South Ward, York, Pennsylvania; Roll: M432_839; Page: 74B; Image: 722.

261 Michael Oberland, 1798, #3, York County Births 1730-1900, Humphrey, Gert Mysliwski,gert@foothill.net.

262 Michael Oberland, St. Matthews Lutheran Church records, Hanover, PA, Helda Kline.

263 Warner family information, JWerner.txt, Don Varner, DRVarner@aol.com.

264 Maria Catharina Werner, baptismal record, St Jacobs Lutheran Church, Vicki Kessler, Secretary, saintjacobslutheranchurch@msn.com.

265 Gipe Family of Chanceford Twp., York Co, 1997, Harry A. Diehl, p 1-5.266 William Anderson, FHL, Pedigree chart, www.familysearch.com.

267 William Anderson, February, 1840, Abstracts of Wills, Chapman, PA.

268 Anderson family information, Bob Anderson, PA, rmorris@ptd.net.

269 Anderson family information, Lisa betts, betts@sprintmail.com.

270 Catharina Arnold, Reformed Church Records in Eastern Pennsylvania, Copied by Dr. William J. Hinke, Church Records of Zion's or Stone Valley Lutheran and Reformed Church, http://www.mahantongo.org.

271 Arnold family, FHL, Pedigree Chart, Ancestral File, www.familysearch.org.

272 Bordner family information, Roger Cramer, rogercubs@aol.com.

273 Descendants of Philip Jacob Bortner, John Getz, jgetz@iu.net.

274 Children of Johann Michael Emerich, The Bordner & Burtner Families, H.W. Bordner, Washington DC, 1967, p 10.

275 Emerick family information, Ancestors & Descendants of Johann Michael Emerich of New York 1709-1979, O. S. Emrich, Ann Fenley, Dayton, OH.

276 Gaugler family information, author unknown.

277 Gaugler Notes, Dauphin County Courthouse, Ronald W. Huber, Salfordsville, PA, 1978.

278 Mary Gaugler, Mount Zion United Brethren Church Cemetery, Snyder Co, PA, Shaffer & Arnold, 1904, www.rootsweb.com.

279 Wriah Kelly, Pennsylvania, Death Certificates, 1906-1963 [database on-line]. Provo, UT, USA: Ancestry.com Operations, Inc., 2014.

280 Wm Kelly, Mount Zion United Brethren Church Cemetery, Snyder Co, PA, Shaffer & Arnold, 1904, www.rootsweb.com.

281 Shaffer family information, Debra Kassing, dk2_inc@msn.com.

282 Elizabeth Kelly, Mount Zion United Brethren Church Cemetery, Snyder Co, PA, Shaffer & Arnold, 1904, www.rootsweb.com.

283 Keefer, Kiefer file, Northumberland Co County Historical Society, Sunbury, PA.

284 My Family, Dillon, Kelly, Peterson, etc., Clint Dillon, treegnome@msn.com, awt.ancestry.com.

285 Lycoming County PA & Related Families, Harold E. Bower, Jr., harold.bower@usa.com, awt.ancestry.com.

286 Keefer Book, Pedigree Chart, The Family of Frederick Kieffer, Chapter V, p 1318, E.G. Keefer, 1997.

287 David Kieffer, Union Cemetery Co, Delongs Reformed Church records, Bowers, PA.

288 Peter Kieffer Sr, NSSAR Ecord copy, SAR application, Samuel L Savidge, Northumberland, PA, Nat # 114561, State #8464, Jun 1978.

289 Daniel Keefer, Probate files, 1862, Northumberland County Courthouse, Reg of Wills, Sunbury, Bk 6, p170, PA, Robyn Jackson, genealogylover@msn.com, 2008.

290 John Conrad Bucher, Bucher family, Onetree, ancestry.com.

291 Livezly-Culen marriage record, Gloria Dei Church, 916 S Swanson, Philadelphia, PA 19147, bk 18, p 6.

292 History of Pennsylvania volunteers, 1861-5; prepared in compliance with acts of the legislature, by Samuel P. Bates. Collection: Making of America Books History of Pennsylvania volunteers, 1861-5; prepared in compliance with acts of the legislature, by Samuel P. Bates, 1827-1902.

293 http://155thpa.tripod.com/id2.html - see pictures of the uniforms here.

294 http://civilwar.gratzpa.org/2011/01/tower-city-porter-township-centennial-civil-war-veterans-list/

295 http://civilwar.gratzpa.org/2012/01/alexander-f-thompson-senator-and-attorney/

296 http://civilwar.gratzpa.org/2012/01/alexander-f-thompson-senator-and-attorney/; http://www.findagrave.com/cgi-bin/fg.cgi?page=gr&GRid=117381891

297 http://civilwar.gratzpa.org/2012/01/alexander-f-thompson-senator-and-attorney/

298 http://civilwar.gratzpa.org/2012/04/2012-additions-to-civil-war-veterans-list-g-to-i/

299 http://civilwar.gratzpa.org/veterans/Charles McKean, "Edinburgh: 3. 1750 Onwards" in: The Oxford Companion to Scottish History, Edited by Michael Lynch, OUP, 2007

300 http://coalregionhistorychronicles.blogspot.com/2008/09/explosion-at-york-farm-colliery.html

301 http://en.wikipedia.org/wiki/Ludlow_Massacre

302 http://explorepahistory.com/story.php?storyId=1-9-4

303 http://files.usgwarchives.net/pa/schuylkill/history/local/munsell/hist0012.txt

304 http://files.usgwarchives.net/pa/schuylkill/military/civilwar/captured.txt

305 http://historynewsnetwork.org/article/623

306 http://quod.lib.umich.edu/m/moa/aby3439.0004.001/818?page=root;sid=41cea510eb7635c5b3e50413737b17fb;
size=100;view=image;q1=One+Hundred+And+Fifty-Fifth+Regiment

307 http://quod.lib.umich.edu/m/moa/aby3439.0004.001/818?page=root;sid=41cea510eb7635c5b3e50413737b17fb;
size=100;view=image;q1=One+Hundred+And+Fifty-Fifth+Regiment History of Pennsylvania volunteers, 1861-5; prepared in compliance with acts of the legislature, by Samuel P. Bates. Collection: Making of America Books
http://quod.lib.umich.edu/m/moa/aby3439.0004.001/818?page=root;sid=41cea510eb7635c5b3e50413737b17fb;size=100;view=image;q1=One+Hundred+And+Fifty-Fifth+Regiment.

308 http://ultimatehistoryproject.com/before-the-whiteout-wedding-dresses-and-grooms-outfits.html

309 http://usminedisasters.com/Mine_Disasters/search_Coal_state.asp?ACC_STATE_NAME=Pennsylvania&x=11&y=15

310 http://www.civilwar.org/education/history/warfare-and-logistics/warfare/richmond.html

311 http://www.civilwararchive.com/Unreghst/unpacav1.htm#9th

312 http://www.dailykos.com/story/2013/09/22/1211516/-Sweet-Home-Schuylkill-County-The-PA-Anthracite-coal-region-1790-1917#

313 http://www.dailykos.com/story/2013/09/23/1211516/-Sweet-Home-Schuylkill-County-The-PA-Anthracite-coal-region-1790-1917.

314 http://www.digitalarchives.state.pa.us/archive.asp?view=ArchiveItems&ArchiveID=17&FL=G&FID=1194432&LID=1194481

315   http://www.ebooksread.com/authors-eng/jm-runk--company/commemorative-biographical-encyclopedia-of-dauphin-county-pennsylvania--contai-urm/page-198-commemorative-biographical-encyclopedia-of-dauphin-county-pennsylvania--contai-urm.shtml
316 http://www.findagrave.com/cgi-bin/fg.cgi?page=gr&GRid=62785330
317 http://www.lancasteratwar.com/2011/12/here-comes-cavalry-part-ii-lochiel.html
318 http://www.measuringworth.com/uscompare
319 http://www.measuringworth.com/uscompare/relativevalue.php
320 http://www.pacivilwar.com/regiment/155th.html
321 http://www.pacivilwar.com/regiment/191st.html
322 http://www.pagenweb.org/~schuylkill/castle/castle19.jpg
323 http://www.rootsweb.ancestry.com/~padauph2/lykinsnews.html
324 http://zouavedatabase.weebly.com/civil-war-zouave-unit-master-list.html
325 https://archive.org/stream/troopsundercomma01harr/troopsundercomma01harr_djvu.txt
326
https://books.google.com/books?id=eCk_AQAAMAAJ&pg=PA159&lpg=PA159&dq=Bast+%26+Thompson
+Schuylkill+county+mines&source=bl&ots=CWTape7T1m&sig=Qm3SW59QO91reKpIIeicM0cI0UU&hl
=en&sa=X&ei=9Jj-
VPrtCMu0ggTCrYHgDA&ved=0CC4Q6AEwAw#v=onepage&q=Bast%20%26%Thompson%20
Schuylkill%20county%20mines&f=false
327 https://books.google.com/books?id=j3NWAAAAYAAJ&pg=PA1080&lpg=PA1080&dq=solomon+
updegrove+d.+1864+georgia&source=bl&ots=8iZFQh28Zi&sig=XR_F0FkDZ9F8_9Bp206AZktxp2I&hl=
en&sa=X&ved=0CB8Q6AEwAGoVChMIhbGV5_G7xwIVDOCACh138gBg#v=onepage&q=solomon%2
0updegrove%20d.%201864%20georgia&f=false;   http://www.findagrave.com/cgi-
bin/fg.cgi?page=gr&GRid=84377395
328https://books.google.com/books?id=MTTAAAAIAAJ&pg=PA179&dq=%22daniel+updegrove
%22&hl=en&sa=X&ved=0CC4Q6AEwA2oVChMI_67k2MKnxwIVy6CACh1IaQDu#v=onepage&q=dani
el%20updegrove&f=false, Weekly Notes of Cases Argued and Determined in the Supreme Court ..., Volume
20
329 https://books.google.com/books?id=rRwQAAAAYAAJ&pg=PA308&lpg=PA308&dq=Captain+
John+McMillan%E2%80%99s+company,+Colonel+Fenton%E2%80%99s+regiment,+of+the+Pennsylvani
a+Militia&source=bl&ots=YpSCK5C7sj&sig=hKIwaYSwScmid-HNUo_kavB2_EE&hl=en&sa=X&ei=
_cpfVfnLMczBsAXt-YAI&ved=0CDIQ6AEwBA#v=onepage&q=Captain%20John
%20McMillan%E2%80%99s%20company%2C%20Colonel%20Fenton%E2%80%99s%20regiment%2C%
20of%20the%20Pennsylvania%20Militia&f=false
330 https://books.google.com/books?id=xr-rrOqOPysC&pg=PA553&lpg=PA553&dq=
Lochiel+Cavalry+and+libby+prison&source=bl&ots=31SzP5eI6A&sig=g46Cqj-
M4kAZOwYpx5fCh84j6Oo&hl=en&sa=X&ved=0CEMQ6AEwBmoVChMIgr6vufqnxwIVw4MNCh0ny
A2A#v=onepage&q=Lochiel%20&f=false A Scout to East Tennessee by the Lochiel Cavalry. Anecdotes,
Poetry, and Incidents of the War: North and South: 1860-1865, By Frank Moore
331 https://books.google.com/books?id=zagAAAAYAAJ&printsec=frontcover&source=gbs_ge_
summary_r&cad=0#v=onepage&q=hensel&f=false; After the Reserves: An Unofficial History of the 190th
and 191st Pennsylvania Volunteer Infantry Regiments, June 1, 1864 through June 28, 1865
332 http://www.pareserves.com/files/pdf_files/AFTER%20THE%20RESERVES.PDF Under the Maltese
Cross (1910)
333 https://en.wikipedia.org/wiki/Libby_Prison_Escape
334 https://www.lycoming.edu/umarch/chronicles/2011/2Evangelical.pdf
335 Luther Reily Kelker, History of Dauphin County, Pennsylvania: With Genealogical Memoirs, Volumes
1-2, p. 1080
336 Schuylkill County Firefighting by Michael R. Glore and Michael J. Kitsock. Arcadia Publishing, 2010.
337 The West Schuylkill Herald, Jan 3, 1901, Jeffrey A. Brown, ntrprz@dmv.com
338 Collection: Making of America Books

339 Tower City, Porter Township Centennial book, 1868-1968, Records of Jim Thompson, jbthompson@compuserve.com

340 http://archive.org/stream/lykenswilliamsva00barr/lykenswilliamsva00barr_djvu.txt

341 http://archive.org/stream/lykenswilliamsva00barr/lykenswilliamsva00barr_djvu.txt Harrisburg Patriot Sept. 7, 1891

342 http://archive.org/stream/lykenswilliamsva00barr/lykenswilliamsva00barr_djvu.txt Lykens-Williams Valley directory and pictorial review Map population density of the United States from the 1810 census www.wfu.edu Lykens-Williams Valley directory and pictorial review Annals of Buffalo Valley, Pennsylvania, 1755-1855, Linn, John Blair

343 http://explorepahistory.com/story.php?storyId=1-9-E&chapter=1 (Dauphin from state data)

344 http://www.carnegielibrary.org/research/ Lykens-Williams Valley history - directory and pictorial review

345 http://www.wtwp.org/ Harrisburg Patriot, January 18, 1906 Harrisburg Patriot,

346 http://www.dcnr.state.pa.us/cs/groups/public/documents/document/dcnr_009325.pdf

347 http://www.dcnr.state.pa.us/cs/groups/public/documents/document/dcnr_009325.pdf

348 http://www.dol.gov/dol/aboutdol/history/coalstrike.htm

349 http://www.familysearch.org Harrisburg Patriot, August 23, 1917 Lykens - Williams Valley History Directory J. Allen Barrett ancestry.com

350 http://www.msha.gov/District/Dist_01/History/history.htm

351 http://www.pbs.org/wned/war-of-1812/timeline/ Lykens-Williams Valley history,

352 http://www.portal.state.pa.us/portal/server.pt/community/events/4279/

353 http://www.reviewhttp://archive.org/stream/lykenswilliamsva00barr/lykenswilliamsva00barr_djvu.txt

354 http://www.unioncountyhistoricalsociety.orgAnnals of Buffalo Valley, Pennsylvania, 1755-1855 Linn, John Blair 1850 United States Census Annals of Buffalo Valley, Pennsylvania, 1755-1855 Linn, John Blair Lykens-Williams Valley history - directory and pictorial

355 Brief history of York County PA by George R. Powell; pg 28; copyright 1906

356 Catherine Duncan, Death certificate, Northumberland Co County Register of Wills, Sunbury, PA

357 Charley Duncan, Baptisms of Infants, Zion Evan Luth Register, 1851-1892, Sunbury, PA, p101

358 Charlotte Layman, Duncan family information, Stephanie Gormley

359 County of Northumberland Pennsylvania www.northumberlandco.org

360 David McCloud, Probate files, 1864, Northumberland County Courthouse, Reg of Wills, Sunbury, Bk 5, p261, PA

361 David R. Layman, Biography, source unknown

361 Donkert household, 1880 United States Census, Northumberland Co, PA, ancestry.com & Microfilm, PA State Library, Hbg, PA

363 Duncan death certificate, #0030852, #90924, Northumberland Co, PA, Department of Vital records, New Castle, PA

364 Duncan family information, 1870 United States Census, York Co, PA, Roll M5931468, p 545, Image 700, ancestry.com & Microfilm, PA State Library, Hbg, PA

365 Duncan family information, Jack Lehman, North Charleston, SC

366 Duncan family information, Stephanie Gormley, PA, 1989

367 Duncan household, 1900 United States Census, microfilm image, PA State Library. Died Sunbury, PA,

368 Duncan household, 1900 United States Census, microfilm image, PA State Library

369 Duncan household, 1910 United States Census, Northumberland Co, PA, ED 0118, Visit 0155, ancestry.com & Microfilm, PA State Library, Hbg, PA

370 Duncan-Layman marriage record, #8855, Northumberland Co, PA, 1899, Northumberland Co County Register of Wills, Sunbury, PA

371 Duncan-Layman marriage record, April 20, 1899, Edward C. Eisley

372 Dungan household, 1870 United States Census, Northumberland Co, PA, ancestry.com & Microfilm, PA State Library, Hbg, PA

373 Dungard household, 1870 United States Census, Northumberland Co, PA, ancestry.com & Microfilm, PA State Library, Hbg, PA

374 ED 134, Image 0913, ancestry.com & Microfilm, PA State Library, Hbg, PA

375 Elmira Layman, Bethel ME Cemetery, p 151, Jerome K. Hively, Brogue, PA

376 en.wikipedia.org/wiki/Airville%2C_Pennsylvania

377 files.usgwarchives.net/pa/northumberland/areahistory/bell0011.txt 153 Bell's History of Northumberland County Pennsylvania transcribed by Tony Rebuck for use in USGenWeb Archives pages 309 – 311 & 705 – 707 378 http://en.wikipedia.org"Vikings" and "Scottish trades in early modern era" http://www.portal.state.pa.us/ Pennsylvania history – Independence to Civil War

379 First Electric Light Historical Marker, www.explorepahistory.com/hmarker.php?markerId=1-A-399

380 Hannah Artilla Duncan, Baptisms of Infants, Zion Evan Luth Register, 1851-1892, Sunbury, PA, p94

381 Hawkins household, 1900 United States Census, Northumberland Co, PA, ancestry.com & Microfilm, PA State Library, Hbg, PA.

382 Hawkins household, 1920 United States Census, Cook, IL, ancestry.com & Microfilm, PA State Library, Hbg, PA

383 History of Pennsylvania agriculture http://www.portal.state.pa.us

384 How the Homestead Act Transformed America, www.smithsonianmag.com/history-archaeology/How-the-Homestead-Act-Transformed-America.html

385 http://books.google.com/books?id=X6fhAAAAMAAJ&pg=PA542&lpg=PA542&dq= W.+C.+Calhoun+1901+copper+mine+swindler&sourc   e=bl&ots=V-k0i6JsDx&sig=3BQzIxEdNPol7CaiZS2G3kDiW6g&hl=en&sa=X&ei=ZceEUrLQOqnhiAKNmIHYCg&v ed=0CCwQ6AEwA Q#v=onepage&q=W.%20C.%2cCalhoun%201901%20copper%20mine%20swindler&f=false, The Copper Handbook, Volumes 8, By Horace Jared Stevens, Walter Harvey Weed,

386 http://en.wikipedia.org/ History of Elizabethtown PA

387 http://en.wikipedia.org/Flatboats http://www.distancebetweencities.net/ http://www.houseofnames.com

388 http://en.wikipedia.org/William McKinley 200 http://www.yorkblog.com/ York Furnace Bridge

389 http://files.usgwarchives.net/pa/york/history/gibson/chanceford-twp.txt The Township of Chanceford, York County, PA, B. F. Porter, M. D., 1886 -

390 http://liveauctions.holabirdamericana.com/CO-Copperfield-Fremont-County-1900-Colorado-Copper-Mining-Company-Stock-Certificate-Fenske-C_i10680523 Colorado Copper Mining Co.

391 http://sharing.ancestry.com/3045477?h=16e789

392 http://www.measuringworth.com/ppowerus/, Measuringworth.com

393 http://www.cityofsunbury.com/ Blacksmithing History 1 - http://www.appaltree.net/aba/hist1.htm

394 http://www.cyberdriveillinois.com/GenealogyMWeb/ODPHdeathsearch

395 http://www.cyberdriveillinois.com/GenealogyMWeb/ODPHdeathsearch.1916-

396 http://www.donicht.de/lutheraner.htm Old Lutheran immigration fever,

397 http://www.gdhspa.org/Dover/flood%20of%201884.htm The Inundation of York, Penna: A Graphic Description of the Great Flood: with an Account of the Violent Rain Storm of June 25, 1884 (Google eBook) - F. L. Spangler, York Daily Printing House, 1884 Flood of 1884

398 http://www.gendisasters.com/data1/ny/earthquakes/eastcoast-earthquake-aug1884.htm 1884 August Earthquake 399 http://www.genealogy.com/24_land.html Revolutionary War Bounty Land Grants -

400 http://www.mahantongo.org/mmhps/stoneval.htm a link from the Northumberland Historical Society found on the City of Sunbury website

401 http://www.mahantongo.org/mmhps/stoneval.htm Zion Stone Valley Church

402 http://www.mayoclinic.com Symptoms of nephritis

403 http://www.healthline.com, Symptoms of cystitis

404 http://www.phmc.state.pa.us Pennsylvania Historical Museum Commission

405 http://www.phmc.state.pa.us/ - Lancaster County http://www.padutchcountry.com Marietta, Lancaster Co. PA

406 http://www.portal.state.pa.us Pennsylvania Historical & Museum Commission

407 http://www.portal.state.pa.us/portal/server.pt/community/overview_of_pennsylvania_history/4281 Pennsylvania Historic & Museum Commission -

408http://www.portal.state.pa.us/portal/server.pt/community/pennsylvania%27s_agricultural_history/2584 Pennsylvania Historic & Museum Commission,

409 http://www.wlsessays.net/files/WesterhausEmigrations.pdf The Confessional Lutheran Emigrations from Prussia and Saxony Around 1839,

410 http://www.yorkblog.com/How did they get across the wide Susquehanna when there were no bridges?

411 http://yorkcountypa.gov/History York County PA http://web.archive.org/ — Agriculture in Lancaster PA

Jefferson Copper Mining Co. Colorado - Scripopholy.com

412 http://scripophily.net/jecomicoco19.html

413 John Reiman, York Co, PA Will index, Gert Mysliwski, gert@foothill.net. http://en.wikipedia.org/ — Lancaster County

414 Joseph P Leyman, Evergreen Cemetery, Index files and lot lists, #5435, Lot SG 157, Maple Gr Pt 6, vault 5/9/box, permit #4976, Chicago, IL

415 Joseph Pierce Layman, death record, Illinois Statewide Death Index, 1916-

416 Joseph Pierce Layman, State of IL, Dept of Public Health, DVS, Reg #4976, Primary Dt #3104, Cook, IL, Feb 1924.

417 Klein household, 1820 United States Census, Lancaster Co, PA, ancestry.com & Microfilm, PA State Library, Hbg, PA

418 Layman household, 1800 United States Census, Centre Co, PA, ancestry.com & Microfilm, PA State Library, Hbg, PA

419 Layman/Lehman family information, Files, NCHS, The Hunter House, Sunbury, PA

420 Laymen household, 1910 United States Census, Northumberland Co, PA, ED 0114, Visit 0085, ancestry.com & Microfilm, PA State Library, Hbg, PA

421 Laynon household, 1900 United States Census, Northumberland Co, PA, ancestry.com & Microfilm, PA State Library, Hbg, PA

422 Lehman-Klein marriage record, June 28, 1818, Church Book records 4

423 Lehman-Klein marriage record, Marriages at Trinity Lutheran Church, Lancaster Co, PA, Joan E. Kahler, Charles.Kahler@worldnet.att.net.

424 Lehman-Oberlander marriage, source unknown

425 Leyman family information, source unknown

426 Lottie Duncan, Pomfret Manor Cemetery, Sam Derr, Sunbury, PA, lot 130-B

427 Lottie V Willard death certificate, File #29987, Reg #19, #3505042, February 1936, Department of Vital Records, New Castle, PA

428 Lottie V. Willard, Lottie Duncan, Pomfret Manor Cemetery, Sam Derr, Sunbury, PA, lot 130-B

429 Lyman household, 1850 United States Census, York Co, PA, Roll M432-

430 Lyman household, 1860 United States Census, York Co, PA, ancestry.com & Microfilm, PA State Library, Hbg, PA

431 Lyman household, 1870 United States Census, York Co, PA, Roll M593 1468, p 545, Image 700, ancestry.com & Microfilm, PA, State Library, Hbg, PA

432 Lyman household, 1880 United States Census, York Co, PA, FHL 1255208, Film T9-1208, p 640D, www.familysearch.org

433 McCloud household, 1860 United States Census, Northumberland Co, PA, Series M653, Roll 1149, p 71, ancestry.com & Microfilm, PA State Library, Hbg, PA

434 McCloud household, 1870 United States Census, Northumberland Co, PA, ancestry.com & Microfilm, PA State Library, Hbg, PA

435 McCloud household, 1880 United States Census, Northumberland Co, PA, ancestry.com & Microfilm, PA State Library, Hbg, PA

436 McCloud-Frye, Marriage, Northumberland County, SS, #2856, Register & Recorder, Sunbury, PA, Oct 1890, Market St, Sunbury, PA.

437 McLeod household, 1850 United States Census, Northumberland Co, PA, ancestry.com & Microfilm, PA State Library, Hbg, PA

438 Melinda Duncan, Cemetery record, Apr 1933, A genealogists Guide to Burials in Northumberland Co, PA, Vol I, Meiser & Meiser, 1989

439 Michael Layman, Bethel ME Cemetery, p 151, Jerome K. Hively, Brogue, PA

440 National Heart and Lung Institute, What Causes Pneumonia? www.nhlbi.nih.gov

441 Layman Family information from Marc Thompson

442 Northumberland Co County Register of Wills

443 Oberlander household, 1830 United States Census, York Co, PA, ancestry.com & Microfilm, PA State Library, Hbg, PA

444 Oberlander household, 1840 United States Census, York Co, PA, ancestry.com & Microfilm, PA State Library, Hbg, PA

445 Oberlander household, 1850 United States Census, York Co, PA, Roll M432 839, p 839, ancestry.com & Microfilm, PA State Library, Hbg, PA

446 Oberlander household, 1860 United States Census, York Co, PA, ancestry.com & Microfilm, PA State Library, Hbg, PA

447 Oberlander household, 1870 United States Census, York Co, PA, ancestry.com & Microfilm, PA State Library, Hbg, PA

448 Oberlander household, 1880 United States Census, York Co, PA, FHL 1255207, Film T9-1207, p 599C, www.familysearch.org

449 Sarah Oberlander, Overlander-Kipe marriage record, #662-59, Calendar of Vital Records of the Counties of York & Adams

450 Pennsylvania in the Civil War www.wikipedia.org Brief history of York County PA by George R. Powell; pg 28; copyright 1906

451 Pennsylvania, 1851-92, Zion Evangelical Church, www.ancestry.com William Duncan, Baptisms of Infants, Zion Evan Luth Register, 1851-1892, Sunbury, PA, p41

452 Probate files, 1874, Rep 42, Bk 342, York County Archives, York, PA, Deborah Hershey, Elizabethtown, PA, Dec 2008

453 Rebecca Layman, Pomfret Manor Cemetery, Sam Derr, Sunbury, PA, lot 130-B

454 Rebecca Lehman (Layman) death certificate, #105066, Reg # 456, #3457529, November 1921, Department of Vital Records, New Castle, PA

455 Rieman household, 1820 United States Census, York Co, PA, ancestry.com & Microfilm, PA State Library, Hbg, PA

456 Robyn Jackson, genealogylover@msn.com, 2008

457 Sallie Duncan, Cemetery record, Apr 1933, A genealogists Guide to Burials in Northumberland Co, PA, Vol I, Meiser & Meiser, 1989

458 Sarah Duncan, Baptisms of Infants, Zion Evan Luth Register, 1851-1892, Sunbury, PA, p41

459 Sarah Oberlander, Probate files, 1874, Rep 42, York County Archives, York, PA, Deborah Hershey, Elizabethtown, PA, Dec 2008.

460 wiki.answers.com/Q/Why_did_people_leave_Germany_for_America_in_the_late_1800's?

461 Willard household, 1920 United States Census, Northumberland Co, PA, Roll T625 1611, p 7A, ED 134, Image 0913, ancestry.com & Microfilm, PA State Library, Hbg, PA

462 Willard household, 1930 United States Census, Northumberland Co, PA, Roll T626 2091, p 7A, ED 71, Image 0681, ancestry.com & Microfilm, PA State Library, Hbg, PA

463 William Duncan, Baptisms of Infants, Zion Evan Luth Register, 1851-1892, Sunbury, PA, p41

464 William Duncan, Northumberland Co County, Pennsylvania, 1851-92, Zion Evangelical Church, www.ancestry.com

465 William Duncan, Pomfret Manor Cemetery, Sam Derr, Sunbury, PA, lot 130-B

466 William Duncan, Pomfret Manor Cemetery, Sunbury, Northumberland Co, PA, NCHS, The Hunter House, Sunbury, PA

467 William Duncan, Probate files, July 1906, Northumberland County Courthouse, Reg of Wills, Bk 12, p424, Sunbury, PA, Robyn Jackson, genealogylover@msn.com, 2008

468 William Duncan, Probate files, July 1906, Northumberland County Courthouse, Reg of Wills, Bk 12, p424, Sunbury, PA, Robyn Jackson, genealogylover@msn.com, 2008.

469 Duncan family information, Jack Lehman, North Charleston, SC

470 Wm Duncan death certificate, #0030852, #90924, Northumberland Co, PA, Department of Vital records, New Castle, PA

471 Wm Duncan, Northumberland Co County Courthouse, Register of Wills, 11-27-1901

472 http://cigarhistory.info/Cigar_History/History_1878-1915.html

473 http://en.wikipedia.org/wiki/Dyeing
474 http://en.wikipedia.org/wiki/History_of_cancer
475 http://en.wikipedia.org/wiki/Pennsylvania
476 http://en.wikipedia.org/wiki/Pennsylvania_Canal
477 http://en.wikipedia.org/wiki/Samuel_Gompers
478 http://en.wikipedia.org/wiki/Snyder_County,_Pennsylvania
479 http://explorepahistory.com/story.php?storyId=1-9-10
480 http://explorepahistory.com/story.php?storyId=1-9-21
481 http://www.allentownsd.org/Page/16
482 http://www.ancestry.com/name-origin?surname=bordner
483 http://www.ancestry.com/name-origin?surname=gaugler
484 http://www.phme.state.pa.us/bhp/AQL/context/Central_Limestone_Valleys.pdf
485 http://en.wikipedia.org/wiki/Pennsylvania_Lumber_Museum
486 http://www.princeton.edu/history/people/display_person.xml?netid=hartog&interview=yes
487 http://www.prrths.com
488 http://www.shmoop.com/1920s/economy.html
489 http://www.wiley.com/legacy/products/subject/business/forbes/ford.html
490 http://en.wikipedia.org/wiki/Rural_electrification#United_States
491 http://zerbetownship.org/history.asp
492 http://en.wikipedia.org/wiki/Ashland,_Pennsylvania
493 http://en.wikipedia.org/wiki/Brakeman
494 http://en.wikipedia.org/wiki/Federal_Employers_Liability_Act
495 http://www.pinegrovetownship.com/History.html
496 http://www.questia.com/library/history/social-history/women-in-19th-century-america
497 http://www.answers.com/topic/sewing-machine
498 http://www.answers.com/topic/clothing-industry
499 http://www.nps.gov/civilwar/search-regiments-detail.htm?regiment_id=UPA0172RIX 32
500 http://en.wikipedia.org/wiki/Pennsylvania_in_the_American_Civil_War
501 http://www.etymonline.com/cw/draft.htm
502 http://en.wikipedia.org/wiki/Militia_%28United_States%29#Civil_War
503 http://en.wikipedia.org/wiki/Peninsula_Campaign
504 http://en.wikipedia.org/wiki/History_of_education_in_the_United_States#One-room_schoolhouses
505 http://en.wikipedia.org/wiki/Port_Trevorton,_Pennsylvania
506 http://www.portal.state.pa.us/portal/server.pt/community/pennsylvania%27s_agricultural_history/2584
507 http://www.portal.state.pa.us/portal/server.pt/community/pennsylvania%27s_agricultural_history/2584/
North_and_West_Branch.pdf
508 http://relationships.blurtit.com/1647575/what-was-the-average-family-size-in-the-19th-century
509 http://en.wikipedia.org/wiki/Pennsylvania_in_the_American_Civil_War
510 http://en.wikipedia.org/wiki/Shamokin_%28village%29
511 http://en.wikipedia.org/wiki/Sunbury,_Pennsylvania
512 http://en.wikipedia.org/wiki/Pennsylvania_Canal
513 http://en.wikipedia.org/wiki/File:Pennsylvania_canals.png
514 http://en.wikipedia.org/wiki/Main_Line_of_Public_Works
515 http://en.wikipedia.org/wiki/Pennsylvania_Railroad
516 http://explorepahistory.com/story.php?storyId=1-9-10
517 http://hatbox.com/hat-history.cfm 50 http://en.wikipedia.org/wiki/Mad_hatter_disease
518 http://en.wikipedia.org/wiki/History_of_the_Ursulines_in_New_Orleans
519 http://en.wikipedia.org/wiki/Ashland,_Pennsylvania
520 http://www.rootsweb.ancestry.com/~wibrown/naming.htm

CURRY SOURCES

1   Eddie Mazo, December 1997, GA, Social Security Death Index, www.ancestry.com.

2   Eddie Mazo, Certificate of Death, #054861, Sumter, GA, State Registrar, Atlanta, GA.

3   Delored Curry death certificate, #124-544, February, 1948, Chatham, GA, State Office of Vital Records.

4   Kressie Joe Curry, Birth register, no name, 2-23-1948, Vital records, Chatham Co Health Dept, PO Box 14257, Savannah, GA.

5   Eddie Mazo, December 1997, GA, Social Security Death Index, www.ancestry.com.

6   Ned Mason, Certificate of Death, #054861, Sumter, GA, State Registrar, Atlanta, GA.

7   Mr. Eddie Mazo, Sect I, # 682, United States Dept. of the Interior, NSP, Andersonville National Historical Site, Andersonville, GA, Gerry Allen.

8   Jones household, 1920 United States Federal Census, Fulton, GA, ancestry.com &Microfilm, PA State Library, Hbg, PA.

9   Bank household, 1900 United States Census, Jefferson, AL, ancestry.com & Microfilm, PA State Library, Hbg, PA.

10   Eddie Mazo, United States WW II Army Enlistment Records, 1938-1946, NARA, www.ancestry.com.

11   Mr. Eddie Mazo, United States Dept. of the Interior, NSP, Andersonville National Historical Site, Andersonville, GA, Gerry Allen.

12   Eddie Mazo, United States World War II Army Enlistment Records, 1938-1946, NARA,www.ancestry.com.

13   Delores Curry death certificate, #124-544, February, 1948, Chatham, GA, State Office of Vital Records.

14   Mack Mason, Social Security numident record, application for SS-5, SSA, Nov 2006, Baltimore, MD.

15   Mack Mason death certificate, #24230, #1271, September 1962, Chatham, GA, State Office of VitalRecords.

16   Mack Mason Sr. death certificate, #24230, September 1962, Georgia Deaths 1919-98, Chatham, GA, www.ancestry.com, Kathryn Gordon Hamby.

17   Mack Mason Sr, GA Deaths, 1919-1998, #24230, www.ancestry.com.

18   Mason-Thompson marriage, State of Georgia, Washington Co, Marriage license, Washington Co Probate Court, 1902.

19   Mason household, 1910 United States Census, Jefferson, GA, ancestry.com & Microfilm, PA State Library, Hbg, PA.

20   Mason-Thompson marriage, Wash. Co Marriage Records, State of Georgia, Washington Co, Washington Co Probate Court, 1902, Book I, #519.

21   More household, 1900 United States Census, Washington Co, GA, ancestry.com &Microfilm, PA State Library, Hbg, PA.

22   Mason household, 1900 United States Census, Washington, GA, ancestry.com & Microfilm, PA State Library, Hbg, PA.

23   Mason household, 1920 United States Census, Jefferson, GA, www.ancestry.com, Kathryn Gordon Hamby.

24   Mason household, 1930 United States Census, Chatham Co, GA, ancestry.com & Microfilm, PA State Library, Hbg, PA.

25   Mason household, 1910 United States Census, Washington, GA, ancestry.com & Microfilm, PA State Library, Hbg, PA.

26   Mason household, 1930 United States Census, Chatham, GA, ancestry.com & Microfilm, PA State Library, Hbg, PA.

27   Mack Mason, 258-34-9996, SS-5, Application for SSA Number, Baltimore, MD.

28   Mack Mason, Jeff. Co Tax Digest 1907, Office of Probate Court, Jeff. Co, Courthouse, Louisville, GA.

29   Mason household, 1920 United States Census, Jefferson, GA, www.ancestry.com, Kathryn Gordon Hamby.

30   Mack Mason, September 1962, GA, Social Security Death Index, www.ancestry.com.

31   Shatteen household, 1900 United States Census, Washington Co, GA, ancestry.com &Microfilm, PA State Library, Hbg, PA.

32   Mason household, 1920 United States Census, Jefferson, GA, ancestry.com & Microfilm, PA State Library, Hbg, PA.

33   Mason household, 1920 United States Census, Chatham, GA, ancestry.com & Microfilm, PA State Library, Hbg, PA.

34   Robert Forsythe, SS-5 application, Application for SSN, Social Security Administration, 1945.

35   Forsyth-Curry marriage, Marriage License, State of GA, Chatham County, April 17, 1948.

36   Robert Forsythe, Robert Forsythe, United States Veterans Cemeteries, ca. 1800-2006,Tahoma Nat'l Cemetery, NCA, Provo, UT, myfamily.com, Inc., 2006, www.ancestry.com.

37   Robert Forsythe, Social Security Death Index, Provo, UT, 259-40-7505, www.ancestry.com.

38   Forsyth-Curry marriage, Marriage License, State of GA, Chatham County, April 17, 1948.

39   Cressie Curry, December 1998, issued PA, resided GA, Social Security Death Index, www.ancestry.com.

40   Forsyth-Curry marriage, Marriage License, State of GA, Chatham County, April 17, 1948. #059026, January 14, 1999, Georgia State Office of Vital Records, GA.

41   Cressie Curry death certificate, #059026, January 14, 1999, Georgia State Office of Vital Records, GA.

42   Robert Forsythe, Social Security numident record, application for SS-5, SSA, Nov 2006, Baltimore, MD.

43   Robert Forsythe, United States Veterans Cemeteries, ca. 1800-2006,Section J, Row B, site 85, Tahoma Nat'l Cemetery, NCA, Provo, UT, myfamily.com, Inc., 2006, www.ancestry.com.

44   Dunham household, 1930 United States Census, Chatham Co, GA, ancestry.com & Microfilm, PA State Library, Hbg, PA.

45   Robert Forsythe, United States Veterans Cemeteries, ca. 1800-2006,Tahoma Nat'l Cemetery, NCA, Provo, UT, myfamily.com, Inc., 2006, www.ancestry.com.

46   Nina Washington Forsythe, death certificate, Vitals Records, Ga Dept. of Public Health, 1944,Savannah, Chatham, GA.

47   Robert Forsythe, Tahoma National Cemetery Maple Valley, King County, Washington 18600 Southeast 240th St.
Kent, WA 98042-4868.

48   Elizabeth Curry, Certificate of Death, Custodians #1401, October 1965, Vital records, Chatham Co Health Dept, PO Box 14257, Savannah, GA.

49   Cressie Mazo, SS-5, Application for SSN, 202-40-5156, March 1966, Social Security Administration.

50   Cressie Curry, December 10, 1998, GA, Social Security Death Index, www.ancestry.com.

51   Cressie Curry death certificate, #059026, January 14, 1999, Georgia State Office of Vital Records, GA and Cressie Curry, December 10, 1998, PA, Social Security Death Index, www.ancestry.com.

52   Aggie Palmer, Certificate of Death, Commonwealth of GA, State Board of Health, File#9966, Ivey, GA, Mar 1922.

53   Mason household, 1900 United States Census, Washington, GA, ancestry.com & Microfilm, PA State Library, Hbg, PA.

54   Mason household, 1870 United States Census, Washington, GA, ancestry.com & Microfilm,P A State Library, Hbg, PA.

55   Mason household, 1880 United States Census, Washington, GA, ancestry.com & Microfilm ,PA State Library, Hbg, PA.

56   Mason household, 1880 United States Census, Washington, GA, FHL 1254171, Film T9-0171, p 360B, www.familysearch.org.

57   Mason household, 1870 United States Census, Washington, GA, ancestry.com & Microfilm, PA State Library, Hbg, PA.

58   Edward Mason, 1888, Savannah, GA Directories, 1888-91, www.ancestry.com.

59   Mason household, 1870 United States Census, Washington, GA, Roll M593 182, p 261, Image199, ancestry.com & Microfilm, PA State Library, Hbg, PA.

60   Mason household, 1880 United States Census, Washington, GA, Roll T9-171, Film 1254171,p 360B, ED 129, Image 0102, ancestry.com & Microfilm, PA State Library, Hbg, PA.

61   Aggie Palmer, Certificate of Death, Commonwealth of GA, State Board of Health, File#9966, Ivey, GA, Mar 1922.

62   Mason-Wicker, Marriage license, State of Georgia, Washington County, Probate court, Sandersville, GA.

63   Mason-Clayton, Marriage license, State of Georgia, Washington County, Probate court, Sandersville, GA.

64   Thompson household, 1900 United States Census, Jefferson Co, GA, ancestry.com & Microfilm, PA State Library, Hbg, PA.

65   Thompson-Shatteen, marriage license, State of GA, Washington Co, Marriage records bk E, p 281, 1879-1885, Probate court of Washington Co, Sandersville, GA.

66   Annie Thompson, Savannah, Georgia, Cemetery and Burial Records, 1852-1939 about Annie Thompson.

67   Thompson household, 1880 United States Census, Washington Co, GA, ancestry.com &Microfilm, PA State Library, Hbg, PA.

68   Shatteen household, 1880 United States Census, Washington Co, GA, ancestry.com &Microfilm, PA State Library, Hbg, PA.

69   Forsythe household, 1900 United States Census, Duval, FL, ancestry.com & Microfilm, PA State Library, Hbg, PA.

70   Percy Forsythe, Chatham County, GA Probate court, Wills, Estates, Admins, etc., F778, Adm 1942.

71   Nina Washington Forsyth, Cemetery Record, City of Savannah, Cemeteries Dept., Savannah, GA c/o Jerry Flemming, Director of Cemeteries.

72   Nina Forsythe, Chatham County, GA Probate court, Wills, Estates, Admins, etc., F806, Adm 1944.

73   Forsyth household, 1910 United States Census, Duval, FL, ancestry.com & Microfilm, PA State Library, Hbg, PA.

74   Forsythe household, 1930 United States Census, Washington DC, ancestry.com & Microfilm, PA State Library, Hbg, PA.

75   Percy Campbell Forsythe, Naturalization index, NY Southern intentions, Percy Forsyth, 232663,398, fotenote.com.

76   Percy Campbell Forsythe, Mariners killed in WW2, City of Atlanta, www.usmm.org.

77   Percy C Forsythe, US Rosters of World War II Dead, 1939-1945, Merchant Marine, 196897, www.ancestry.com.

78   Robinson household, 1910 United States Census, Chatham Co, GA, ancestry.com & Microfilm,P A State Library, Hbg, PA.

79   Robinson household, 1920 United States Census, Chatham Co, GA, ancestry.com & Microfilm, PA State Library, Hbg, PA.

80   Freddie Curry, Certificate of Death, Custodians #1582, November 1964, Vital records, Chatham Co Health Dept, PO Box 14257, Savannah, GA.

81   Freddie Curry, Social Security numident record, application for SS-5, SSA, Nov 2006, Baltimore, MD.

82   Mack Mason, Chatham County Deaths, Wyonona Burgstiner, wburgstiner@yahoo.com.

83   Curry household, 1930 United States Census, Chatham, GA, T626, 2, 667, www.ancestry.com, GA-Census-lookup-d, Gina.

84   Curry-Brown marriage, Probate Court, Savannah, GA, p 307, bk 2R's, Sept. 17, 1928, application.

85   Elizabeth Curry, Chatham County Deaths, Wyonona Burgstiner, wburgstiner@yahoo.com.

86   No name Curry, Birth register, Dept. of Public Health, Chatam Co, GA, 2/15/07, Dunkin Curria & Betsy.

87   Freddie Curry, Lot 60, Sec B, Cemetery Record, City of Savannah, Cemeteries Dept., Savannah, GA c/o Jerry Flemming, Director of Cemeteries.

88   Curry household, United States Census, 1910, Chatham, GA, ancestry.com & Microfilm, PA State Library, Hbg, PA.

89   Curry household, United States Census, 1920, Chatham, GA, ancestry.com & Microfilm, PA State Library, Hbg, PA.

90   Curry household, 1930 United States Census, Chatham, GA, T626, 2, 667, ancestry.com &Microfilm, PA State Library, Hbg, PA.

91   Curry household, 1930 United States Census, Chatham, GA, ancestry.com & Microfilm, PA State Library, Hbg, PA.

92   Elizabeth Curry, Lot 60, Sec B, Cemetery Record, City of Savannah, Cemeteries Dept., Savannah, GA c/o Jerry Flemming, Director of Cemeteries.

93   Brown household, 1920 United States Census, Allendale Co, GA, ancestry.com & Microfilm ,PA State Library, Hbg, PA.

94   Mrs.. Elizabeth Curry, Savannah Morning News, Oct 17, 1965, Wyonona Burgstiner,wburgstiner@yahoo.com.

95   Neal household, 1880 United States Census, Washington, GA, ancestry.com & Microfilm, PA State Library, Hbg, PA.

96   Mason-Walker, Marriage license, State of Georgia, Washington County, Probate court, Sandersville, GA.

97   Mason-Adams, Marriage license, State of Georgia, Washington County, Probate court, Sandersville, GA.

98   Mason-Andrews, Marriage license, State of Georgia, Washington County, Probate court, Sandersville, GA.

99   Mason-Moffett, Marriage license, State of Georgia, Washington County, Probate court, Sandersville, GA.

100   Mason-Cumming, Marriage license, State of Georgia, Washington County, Probate court, Sandersville, GA.

101   Brown household, 1870 United States Census, Washington Co, GA, ancestry.com &Microfilm, PA State Library, Hbg, PA.

102   Thompson household, 1870 United States Census, Chatham Co, GA, ancestry.com & Microfilm, PA State Library, Hbg, PA.

103   Thomson household, 1880 US Federal Census, SD 3, ED 36, pg 11, Chatham, GA, p732,www.ancestry.com.

104   Thompson-Mason, Marriage license, State of Georgia, Washington County, Probate court, Sandersville, GA.

105   Thompson-Key, Marriage license, State of Georgia, Washington County, Probate court, Sandersville, GA.

106   Sallie Shateen, Cert of Death, File #26470, Reg #1516, 11/10/1927, GA Virtual Vault,http://content.sos.state.ga.us/cdm4/gadeaths.php.

107   Sallie Shateen, Georgia Deaths, 1919-98, Chatham Co, GA, 1927, www.ancestry.com.

108   Shattine household, 1910 United States Census, Jefferson Co, GA, ancestry.com & Microfilm, PA State Library, Hbg, PA.

109   Shatteen household, 1920 United States Census, Chatham Co, GA, ancestry.com & Microfilm, PA State Library, Hbg, PA.

110   Shatteen-Hall, Marriage license, State of Georgia, Washington County, Probate court, Sandersville, GA.

111   Theophilus Forsythe, Cert of Death, File #05483, Reg #130, 5/23/1919, GA Virtual Vault,http://content.sos.state.ga.us/cdm4/gadeaths.php.

112   Washington household, 1900 United States Census, Beaufort Co, SC, ancestry.com & Microfilm, PA State Library, Hbg, PA.

113   Joe Washington Jr, certificate of death, Beaufort, SC, 1922, South Carolina DHEC, Columbia, SC.

114   Joe Washington, Georgia, Deaths Index, 1914-1927 about Joe Washington, ancestry.com.

115   Robinson household, 1910 United States Census, Chatham, GA, ancestry.com & Microfilm, PA State Library, Hbg, PA.
116   Mary Washington, death record, Georgia Deaths, 1919-98, #7748, www.ancestry.com.
117   Washington household, 1870 United States Federal Census for Fortune Washington, ancestry.com.
118   Washington (Tennia) household, 1880 United States Census, Beaufort Co, SC, www,ancestry.com.
119   Washington (DC) household, 1880 United States Census, Beaufort Co, SC, www,ancestry.com.
120   Washington household, 1910 United States Census, Beaufort Co, SC, www,ancestry.com.
121   Washington household, 1900 United States Census, Beaufort Co, SC, www,ancestry.com.
122   Mary Washington, Laurel Grove Cemetery, Jerry Flemming, Director of Cemeteries, Savannah, GA.
123   Robinson household, 1880 United States Census, Beaufort Co, SC, ancestry.com & Microfilm, PA State Library, Hbg, PA.
124   Robinson household, 1920 United States Census, Chatham, GA, ancestry.com & Microfilm, PA State Library, Hbg, PA.
125   Dunham household, 1930 United States Census, Chatham, GA, ancestry.com & Microfilm, PA State Library, Hbg, PA.
126   Curry household, 1900 United States Census, Chatham, GA, ancestry.com & Microfilm, PA State Library, Hbg, PA.
127   Rosa Louise Curry, Certificate of Death, Commonwealth of GA, State Board of Health, File#13727, Chatham, GA, June 1922.
128   Henry Curry, Chatham County Deaths, Wyonona Burgstiner, wburgstiner@yahoo.com.
129   Duncan Curry, Death Register, June 1914, Chatham County Health Dept., Savannah, GA.
130   Bessie Curry, Georgia Deaths, 1919-98 about Bessie Curry, ancestry.com.
131   Duncan Curry, death certificate, Chatham, GA, Physician's Certificate of the Cause of death, June 1914, CCHD, Savannah, GA.
132   Curry household, United States Census, 1870, Beaufort Co, SC, ancestry.com & Microfilm, PA State Library, Hbg, PA.
133   Curry household, United States Census, 1880, Hampton, SC, ancestry.com & Microfilm, PA State Library, Hbg, PA.
134   Duncan Curry, Savannah, GA Directories, 1888-91, Provo, UT, myfamily.com, Inc.,2001, www.ancestry.com.
135   Colored boy, Birth Certificate, January 1909, Vital records, Chatham Co Health Dept, PO Box 14257, Savannah, GA.
136   Bessie Curry, Savannah, Georgia, Cemetery Burial Lot Cards, 1807-1995 about Bessie Curry, ancestry.com.
137   Alston household, 1880 United States Census, Hampton, SC, ancestry.com & Microfilm, PA State Library, Hbg, PA.
138   Curry household, 1940 United States Federal Census about Willy Curry, ancestry.com.
139   Joe Brown, U.S. World War 1 Draft Registration Cards, No 209, 39-1-3, Allendale, SC, 1942, www.ancestry.com.
140   Colored boy, birth certificate, April 1908, Chatham County Health Dept, Savannah, GA.
141   Joe Brown, Georgia Deaths, 1919-98 about Joe Brown, ancestry.com.
142   Nancy Brown, Georgia Deaths, 1919-98 about Nancy Brown, ancestry.com.
143   Brown household, 1900 United States Census, Barnwell Co, GA, ancestry.com & Microfilm, PA State Library, Hbg, PA.
144   Brown household, 1910 United States Census, Barnwell Co, GA, ancestry.com & Microfilm, PA State Library, Hbg, PA.
145   Brown household, United States Census, 1930, Chatham, GA, ancestry.com & Microfilm, PA State Library, Hbg, PA.
146   Brown household, 1940 United States Federal Census about Joe Brown, ancestry.com.
147   Frazier household, 1900 United States Census, Barnwell Co, GA, ancestry.com & Microfilm, PA State Library, Hbg, PA.

148   Frazier household, 1910 United States Census, Barnwell Co, GA, ancestry.com & Microfilm, PA State Library, Hbg, PA.

149   Houston household, 1870 United States Federal Census about Rhinor Brown, ancestry.com.

150   Robinson household, 1870 United States Census, Beaufort Co, SC, ancestry.com & Microfilm, PA State Library, Hbg, PA.

151   Robinson household, 1900 United States Census, Charleston, SC, www.amcestry.com.

152   Alston household, 1900 United States Census, Chatham, GA, www.amcestry.com.

153   Ben Alston, Savannah, Georgia Vital Records, 1803-1966 about Ben Alston, www.ancestry.com.

154   Ben Alston, Laurel Grove Cem listing, Jerry Flemming, Director of Cemetery, Savannah, GA, Jerry_Flemming@SavannahGa.Gov.

155   Ben Alston, U.S., Find A Grave Index, 1700s-Current about Ben Alston, ancestry.com.

156   Allston household, 1870 United States Census, Beaufort Co, SC, ancestry.com & Microfilm, PA State Library, Hbg, PA.

157   Alston household, 1910 United States Census, Chatham, GA, ancestry.com & Microfilm, PA State Library, Hbg, PA.

158   Alston household, 1880 United States Census, Beaufort Co, SC, ancestry.com & Microfilm, PA State Library, Hbg, PA.

159   Benjamin Alston, Savannah, GA Directories, 1888-91, Provo, UT, myfamily.com, Inc.,2001, www.ancestry.com.

160   Alston household, 1880 United States Census, Lawnton, SC, ancestry.com & Microfilm, PA State Library, Hbg, PA.

161   Brown household, 1880 United States Federal Census about Joseph Brown, ancestry.com.

162   Glover household, 1880 United States Federal Census for Lena Glover, ancestry.com.

163   Samuel Frazier, Georgia Deaths, 1919-1998, ancestry.com.

164   Eva Frazier, Certificate of Death, January 1929, Chatham County Health Dept, State file #2, Savannah, GA.

165   Eva Frazier, Georgia Deaths, 1919-1998, ancestry.com.

166   Sam Frazier, death certificate, Chatham, GA, Local registrar's record of death, March 1928, CCHD, Savannah, GA.

167   Fraisier household, 1870 United States Census, Barnwell Co, GA, ancestry.com & Microfilm, PA State Library, Hbg, PA.

168   Fraser household, 1880 United States Census, Barnwell Co, GA, ancestry.com & Microfilm, PA State Library, Hbg, PA.

169   Frazier household, 1920 United States Census, Allendale Co, GA, ancestry.com & Microfilm, PA State Library, Hbg, PA.

170   Eva Frazier, Cemetery Record, City of Savannah, Cemeteries Dept., Savannah, GA c/o Jerry Flemming, Director of Cemeteries.

171   Thompson household, 1870 United States Census, Barnwell Co, GA, ancestry.com & Microfilm, PA State Library, Hbg, PA.

172   Brown household, 1870 United States Federal Census for David Brown, ancestry.com.

173   Brown household, 1880 United States Federal Census about David Brown, ancestry.com.

174   Hicks household, 1870 United States Federal Census for Milly Hay, ancestry.com.

175   Glover household, 1900 United States Federal Census about Lucia Glover, ancestr.com.

176   Dunbar household, 1900 United States Census, Barnwell Co, SC, ancestry.com & Microfilm, PA State Library, Hbg, PA.

177   Harley household, 1870 United States Federal Census for Lucia Harley, ancestry.com.

ROMANO SOURCES

1   Romano family information, Mary Ann Marchese, Milton, NY.
2   Romano-McCabe marriage certificate, Marriage License Bureau, City of New York, NY Dept of Health, New York, NY, Reg #__911, M027894.
3   Paul Romano, October 1981, NY, Social Security Death Index, www.familysearch.org.
4   Paul Romano death certificate, Cert # 156-81-412485, October 1981, NYC Vital Records, New York, NY.
5   Romano-McCabe marriage certificate, #211012, 16911, Manhattan, New York, NY, 1933.
6   Romano household, 1920 United States Census, Manhattan, New York, NY, www.ancestry.com,Helene Carson and 1920 United States Census, Manhattan, New York, NY, Roll T625 1207, p 5A, ED 906, Image 0676, www.ancestry.com.
7   Romano (Romans) household, 1930 United States Census, New York, NY, ancestry.com & Microfilm, PA State Library, Hbg, PA.
8   Romano household, 1920 United States Census, Manhattan, New York, NY, Roll T625 1207, p5A, ED 906, Image 0676, ancestry.com & Microfilm, PA State Library, Hbg, PA.
9   Paul Romano death certificate, #156-81-412485, October 1981, NYC Vital Records, New York, NY.
10   Paolo Romano, 1914, Martha Washington, Ellis Island Passenger Arrivals: AFIHC, manifest 0008, www.ellisisland.org.
11   Paul Romano, Issued August 12, 1937, March 17, 1938, Proof of Certificated on Citizenship, tag #588012, certificate #4215338, petition #291903.
12   Paul Romano, Social Security numident record, application for SS-5, SSA, Nov 2006, Baltimore, MD.
13   Paul Romano death certificate, 125-05-6041A, Cert # 156-81-412485, October 1981, NYC Vital Records, New York, NY.
14   McCabe household, 1930 United States Census, Manhattan, New York, NY, ancestry.com &Microfilm, PA State Library, Hbg, PA.
15   Kathleen Romano, Obituary, Harrisburg Patriot News.
16   Kathleen Romano, Social Security numident record, application for SS-5, SSA, Nov 2006, Baltimore, MD.
17   Kathleen Romano, Western Union telegram, Harry J Worthing, Pilgrim State Hospital, Brentwood, Suffolk, NY.
18   Kathleen Stewart, October 1, 1997, PA, Social Security Death Index, www.familysearch.org.
19   Kathleen Romano, October 1, 1997, PA, Social Security Death Index, www.familysearch.org.
20   Connor family information, Pat Connor, Luton, ENG.
21   Martin Connor, New York Passenger Lists, 1820-1957, Microfilm T715, Roll T715-4414, p68, www.ancestry.com.
22   Martin O'Connor, born 1906, death certificate, #0065797, Reg #?0581?, June 1986,Department of Vital records, New Castle, PA & Mt. Zion Cemetery, Monroe, Cumberland Co, PA www.rootsweb.com.
23   Martin J O'Connor death certificate, #0065797, Reg #?0581?, June 1986, Department of Vital records, New Castle, PA.
24   Mary O'Connor, #0065798, Reg #075196, August 1986, Department of Vital records, New Castle, PA.
25   Mary Morrison, New York Passenger Lists, 1820-1957, Microfilm T715, Roll T715-4616, p243, www.ancestry.com.
26   Martin J O'Connor, #0065797, Reg #?0581?, June 1986, Department of Vital records, New Castle, PA.
27   Martin O'Connor, Mt. Zion Cemetery, Monroe, Cumberland Co, PA www.rootsweb.com.
28   O'Connor household, 1930 United States Census, New York, NY, ancestry.com & Microfilm, PA State Library, Hbg, PA.

29   Martin O'Connor, Social Security numident record, application for SS-5, SSA, Nov 2006, Baltimore, MD.

30   Martin OConnor, June 1986, PA, Social Security Death Index, www.familysearch.org.

31   Mary Ann O'Connor, Mt. Zion Cemetery, Monroe, Cumberland Co, PA www.rootsweb.com.

32   Mary OConnor, August 1986, PA, Social Security Death Index, www.familysearch.org.

33   Mary Ann O'Connor, Social Security numident record, application for SS-5, SSA, Nov 2006, Baltimore, MD.

34   Carmona-Romano family information, Daniel Zappala, daniel.zappal@gmail.com, email, Dec 2 2009.

35   Romano household, 1920 United States Census, Manhattan, New York, NY, www.ancestry.com,Helene Carson.

36   Pietro Guiseppe Romano, Publicazioni Di Matrimonio, 1890-1910, 1905, Lercara-Friddi, Italy, LDS, microfilm.

37   Anna Romano, NYC Death Index, www.italiangen.org.

38   Romano household, 1920 United States Census, Manhattan, New York, NY, Roll T625 1207, p5A, ED 906, Image 0676, ancestry.com & Microfilm, PA State Library, Hbg, PA.

39   Paolo Romano, 1914, Martha Washington, Ellis Island Passenger Arrivals: AFIHC, manifest 0002, www.ellisisland.org.

40   Anna Carmona, Mary Ann Marchese, Milton, NY.

41   Anna Carmona, 1914, Martha Washington, Ellis Island Passenger Arrivals: AFIHC, manifest 0003, www.ellisisland.org.

42   Pietro Romano, New York Passenger Lists, 1820-1957, Microfilm T715, Roll T715-2356, p104, www.ancestry.com.

43   Owen McCabe, IGI record, 1871, Cavan, Ireland, Batch C012311, www.familysearch.org.

44   Owen McCabe death certificate, Reg # 1488, #2432, January 1935, NYC Vital Records, New York, NY.

45   Mary Smith, FHL, IGI Individual record, Batch M007090, www.familysearch.com.

46   Mary Smith, FHL, IGI Individual record, Batch C701598, Source 0255936, www.familysearch.org.

47   Mary McCabe death certificate, Reg #685, August 1956, NYC Vital records, New York, NY.

48   Mary Smith, New York Passenger Lists, 1820-1957, Roll M237-525, #1369, www.ancestry.com.

49   McCabe household, 1910 United States Census, New York, NY, SD 1, ED 1025, SN 2, family31, Series T624, Roll 1040, p 123, www.ancestry.com, scanned image.

50   McCabe household, 1920 United States Census, New York, NY, www.ancestry.com, Liz McKinnon.

51   Owen McCabe, 1900, Majestic, Ellis Island Passenger Arrivals: AFIHC, manifest 0007, www.ellisisland.org.

52   McCabe household, 1920 United States Census, New York, NY, www.ancestry.com, Liz McKinnon.

53   McCabe household, McCabe household, 1920 United States Census, New York,www.ancestry.com, Liz McKinnon.

54   McCabe household, 1910 United States Census, New York, NY, SD 1, ED 1025, SN 2, family31, Series T624, Roll 1040, p 123, www.ancestry.com, scanned image.

55   Hooker household, 1900 United States Federal Census, Manhattan, NY, SD 1st NY, ED 870,Sheet 10, ancestry.com & Microfilm, PA State Library, Hbg, PA.

56   Mary Smith, FHL, 1875, Individual Record, www.familysearch.org.

57   Manhattan Hospital, 1920 United States Census, 18th Dt, Manhattan, New York, NY,ancestry.com & Microfilm, PA State Library, Hbg, PA.

58   Manhattan Hospital, 1930 United States Census, Manhattan, New York, NY, ancestry.com &Microfilm, PA State Library, Hbg, PA.

59   John Connor, FHL, IGI Individual record, Batch C701229, Source 010188, www.familysearch.org.

60   Mary Anne Barrett, Baptism, Carrentrila, 09-Feb-1868, Backs/Knockmore RC Reg Baptisms, Vol2, p 49, Mayo Family History Centre, Emniscoe, Ireland.

61   John Connor, Baptism, Lisbrin, 18-May-1864, Ballycastle District Reg Births, vol 1,p 8, Mayo Family History Centre, Emniscoe, Ireland.

62   Connor household, 1901 Leitrim-Roscommon Census, Mayo, Ireland.

63   Patrick Morrison, IGI Individual record, Mar 1871, Batch #C014057, familysearch.org.

64   Patrick Morrison death certificate, #239, #79, June 1911, Births & Deaths Acts 1863-1972, Ireland Vital Records, Dublin, Ireland.

65   Morrison-Gilmartin, Marriage, Bonniconlon Church, 21-Nov-1901, Kilmoreroy Dt Reg Marrs, vol 23, p 45, Mayo Family History Centre, Emniscoe, Ireland.

66   Margaret Kilmartin, Born, Drumsheen, 01-Sep-1873, Kilmoreroy Dt Reg Births, vol 12, p 54,Mayo Family History Centre, Emniscoe, Ireland.

67   Morrison household, 1901 Ireland Census, Leitrim-Roscommon, Sligo, Ireland,www.lietrim-roscommon.com.

68   Patrick Morrison death certificate, #239, #79, June 1911, Births & Deaths Acts 1863-1972, Ireland Vital Records, Dublin, Ireland.

69   Margaret Kilmartin, #014, #0091, July 1873, Births & Deaths Acts 1863-1972, Ireland Vital Records, Dublin, Ireland.

70   Margaret Kilmartin, FHL, 1873, FHL Film 101193, Joe Egan and FHL, IGI Individual record, Batch C701598, Source 0255936, www.familysearch.org.

71   Ireneo Romano, Registri di Nascati, Matrimonio e Morte, Ufficio Archivi e Spazi Etnoanthropologici, Archivio Storico Comunale, via Maqueda, 157, Comune di Palermo.

72   Vitale Felice, Registri di Nascati, Matrimonio e Morte, Ufficio Archivi e Spazi Etnoanthropologici, Archivio Storico Comunale, via Maqueda, 157, Comune di Palermo.

73   Angelo Carmone, Registri di Nascati, Matrimonio e Morte, Ufficio Archivi e Spazi Etnoanthropologici, Archivio Storico Comunale, via Maqueda, 157, Comune di Palermo.

74   Angelo Carmona, Estratto per Riassunto di Atto di Morte, Municipio di Messina, 1909,Murco district, Part II, Series D, Action #5484.

75   Angelo Camone, Defuncti, Matrimoni Records, Girolamo Mazzola, Jun 2007, Archivio Storico Comune di Palermo, archiviopa1@virgilio.it.

76   Marianna Quintavalle, Mary Ann Marchese, Milton, NY].

77   McCabe household, 1901 Ireland Census, Leitrim-Roscommon, www.literim-roscommon.com.

78   Smith-Reilly marriage, Registration of Marriages Act, 1863, Chapel of Potahee, 1867, Office of the Registrar General, Ireland.

79   James Smith, Ireland, Civil Registration Deaths Index, 1864-1958 about James Smith, ancestry.com.

80   Connor household, 1901 Ireland Census, Leitrim-Roscommon, Mayo, Ireland,www.lietrim-roscommon.com.

81   Connor household, Web: Ireland, Census, 1911 about Honoria Connor, ancestry.com.

82   Connor household, 1901 Ireland Census, Leitrim-Roscommon, Sligo, Ireland,www.lietrim-roscommon.com.

83   Barrett household, 1881 England Census, Cheshire, ENG, ancestry.com & Microfilm, PA State Library, Hbg, PA.

84   Barrett household, 1881 England Census, Cheshire, ENG, www.ancestry.com.

85   Thomas Barrett, Baptism, Carrentrila, 27-Feb-1832, Backs/Knockmore RC Reg Baptisms, Vol1, p 93, Mayo Family History Centre, Emniscoe, Ireland.

86   Barrett household, 1901 Ireland Census, Leitrim-Roscommon, Mayo, Ireland,www.lietrim-roscommon.com.

87   Barrett household, 1901 Ireland Census, Leitrim-Roscommon, Sligo, Ireland,www.lietrim-roscommon.com.

88   Gilmartin-Naughten, Marriage, Ballyrmunry, 18-Feb-1854, Kilmoreroy/Ballina RC Reg Marrsvol 2, p 249, Mayo Family History Centre, Emniscoe, Ireland.

89   Anne Naughton, Baptism, Ballacmarry, 30-Nov-1834, Sp. Pat Naughton & Anne Mulloy,Kilmoreroy/Ballina RC Reg Baptisms vol 2, p 52, Mayo Family History Centre, Emniscoe, Ireland.

90   Andrew Gilmartin, Ireland, Select Catholic Marriage Registers, 1775-1912 about Andrew Gilmartin, ancestry.com.

91   "Annie" Gilmartin, 1901 Ireland Census, Sligo, Ireland.

92   Gilmartin Household, 1901 Ireland Census, Leitrim-Roscommon, Sligo, Ireland,www.lietrim-roscommon.com.

93   Giuseppe Romano, Defuncti, Matrimoni Records, Girolamo Mazzola, Jun 2007, Archivio Storico Comune di Palermo, archiviopa1@virgilio.it.

94   Erasmo Vitale, Defuncti, Matrimoni Records, Girolamo Mazzola, Jun 2007, Archivio Storico Comune di Palermo, archiviopa1@virgilio.it.

95   Felice Vitale, Defuncti, Matrimoni Records, Girolamo Mazzola, Jun 2007, Archivio Storico Comune di Palermo, archiviopa1@virgilio.it.

96   Camillo Carmone, Registri di Nascati, Matrimonio e Morte, Ufficio Archivi e Spazi Etnoanthropologici, Archivio Storico Comunale, via Maqueda, 157, Comune di Palermo.

97   Angelo Carmona, Registri di Nascati, Matrimonio e Morte, Ufficio Archivi e Spazi Etnoanthropologici, Archivio Storico Comunale, via Maqueda, 157, Comune di Palermo.

98   Giuseppa Quintavalle, Defuncti, Matrimoni Records, Girolamo Mazzola, Jun 2007, Archivio Storico Comune di Palermo, archiviopa1@virgilio.it.

99   James McCabe, Zander, Owner: spudzy777, ancestry.com.

100   Reilly household, Cavan Co 1821 Census, www.cmcrp.net/OtherCty/Cavan1821-3.htm.

101   Angela Romano, Defuncti, Matrimoni Records, Girolamo Mazzola, Jun 2007, Archivio Storico Comune di Palermo, archiviopa1@virgilio.it.

102   Maria Vitale, Defuncti, Matrimoni Records, Girolamo Mazzola, Jun 2007, Archivio Storico Comune di Palermo, archiviopa1@virgilio.it.

WITTLE SOURCES

1   Albert E Wittle death certificate, #0037357, #118301?, February 1985, Department of Vital records, New Castle, PA.

2   Albert E Wittle Sr, East Harrisburg Cemetery Listing, #59, 7/23/2005, Karl Fox, CAGS.

3   Mildred I Michaels death certificate, #0040459, #017720, February 1985, Department of Vital records, New Castle, PA.

4   Mildred Michael, Social Security Death Index, Snyder, PA, 179-12-3502, Feb 1985, www.ancestry.com.

5   Mildred Irene Stewart, #1794340-1920, 10-31-1920, Dauphin Co, PA, Department of VitalRecords, New Castle, PA.

6   Albert E. Wittle, East Harrisburg Cemetery Co, Harrisburg, PA, Section 42, Lot 56, Space Blk A, Grave 4.

7   Wittle (Witble) household, 1910 United States Census, Dauphin Co, PA, ancestry.com & Microfilm, PA State Library, Hbg, PA.

8   Wittle (Witble) household, 1920 United States Census, Dauphin Co, PA, PA State Library, microfilm image.

9   Wittle (Witble) household, 1930 United States Census, Dauphin Co, PA, Roll T626 2026, p 5A, ED54, Image 0725, ancestry.com & Microfilm, PA State Library, Hbg, PA.

10   Albert E Wittle Sr, Obituary, Harrisburg Patriot News.

11   Albert Wittle, US City Directories, Hbg, PA 1939-1946, www.ancestry.com.

12   Albert E Wittle, Death record, John E Neumyer Funeral Home, Inc, Harrsburg, PA, Patrick O'Brien, Supervisor, 2006.

13   Albert E Wittle, 1930, Harrisburg City Directory, www.ancestry.com.

14   Mildred Wittle Michaels, East Harrisburg Cemetery Co, Harrisburg, PA, Section 19, Lot 74.

15   Stewart household, 1930 United States Census, Cumberland Co, PA, Roll T626 2025, p 13A,ED 54, Image 0897, ancestry.com & Microfilm, PA State Library, Hbg, PA.

16   Mildred Wittle Michaels, Obituary, Harrisburg Patriot News.

17   Amel Acri, 1963, PA, Social Security Death Index, www.ancestry.com.

18   Amel F Acri death certificate, #0041830, #014250-63, February 1963, Department of Vital records, NewCastle, PA.

19   Amel Acri, Holy Cross Burial register, Section G, Block 4, Lot 3S, Grave 2,Diocese of Harrisburg, Harrisurg, PA.

20   Silvia Francesca Barbuscio, Birth Certificate, Ministero per i Beni e le Attivita Culturali, Archivio di Stato di Cosenza, Via Miceli, Cosenza.

21   Sylvia Acri, 1992, PA, Social Security Death Index, www.ancestry.com.

22   Sylvia F Acri death certificate, #0039726, #24096, February 1992, Department of Vital records, New Castle, PA.

23   Aemilius Acri, Sacred Heart of Jesus, microfilm #13, Diocese of Harrisburg, Harrisburg, PA.

24   Amel F. Acri, Holy Cross Cemetery, Catholic Cemeteries, Harrisburg, PA, Section G, Block 4, Lot 3S, Grave 2.

25   Acra household, 1910 United States Census, Dauphin Co, PA, ED 0052, Visit 0065,ancestry.com & Microfilm, PA State Library, Hbg, PA.

26   Acri household, 1920 United States Census, Dauphin Co, PA, Roll T625 1558, p 3A, ED58, Image 0030, www.ancestry.com and 1920 United States Census, Dauphin Co, PA, PA State Library microfilm image.

27   Acra household, 1910 United States Census, Dauphin Co, PA, ED 0052, Visit 0065,ancestry.com & Microfilm, PA State Library, Hbg, PA.

28   Amel F Acri, Holy Cross Cemetery, Catholic Cemeteries, Harrisburg, PA, Section G, Block 4, Lot 3S, Grave 2.

29   Amel F Acri, Obituary, Harrisburg Patriot News.

30   Sylvia F. Acri, Holy Cross Cemetery, Catholic Cemeteries, Harrisburg, PA, Section G, Block 4, Lot 3, Grave 3.

31   Barbush household, 1930 United States Census, Dauphin Co, PA, Roll T626 2026, p 3B, ED22, Image 0612, ancestry.com & Microfilm, PA State Library, Hbg, PA.

32   Barbush household, 1930 United States Census, , PA, Roll T626 2026, p 3B, ED 22, Image0612, ancestry.com & Microfilm, PA State Library, Hbg, PA.

33   Sylvia Acri, Probate files, 1992, Orphans Court Record, 42pp, Dauphin County Courthouse, Reg of Wills, Deborah Hershey, Elizabethtown, PA, Mar 2008.

34   Sylvia F Acri, Obituary, Harrisburg Patriot News.

35   John E Wittle, #0795091, File #52086, Reg # 677, March 1934, PA Vitals Records, New Castle, PA.

36   Wittle-Minnich marriage record, Cumberland County, PA, May 1893, #M-1-493.

37   Mary E Whittle, #1233358, File #28314, Reg # 371, March 1934, PA Vitals Records, New Castle, PA.

38   Whittle household, 1870 United States Census, Dauphin Co, PA, ancestry.com & Microfilm, PA State Library, Hbg, PA.

39   Killian household, 1880 United States Census, Lancaster, PA, Roll T9 1142, Film 1255142, p59A, ED 150, Image 0287, ancestry.com & Microfilm, PA State Library, Hbg, PA.

40   Wittle (Witble) household, 1900 United States Census, Dauphin Co, PA, www.ancestry.com and 1900United States Census, Dauphin Co, PA, Pa State Library microfilm image.

41   Wittle household, 1910 United States Census, Dauphin Co, PA, ancestry.com & Microfilm, PA State Library, Hbg, PA.

42   John E Wittle, #0795091, File #52086, Reg # 677, March 1934, PA Vital Records, New Castle, PA.

43   Wittle (Witble) household, 1887-1900 Harrisburg, PA Directories, www.ancestry.com.

44   Wittle household, 1900 United States Census, Dauphin Co, PA, www.ancestry.com and 1900United States Census, Dauphin Co, PA, Pa State Library microfilm image.

45   John E Wittle, US City Directories, Hbg, PA 1875-1946, www.ancestry.com.

46   Minick household, 1880 United States Census, Dauphin Co, PA, www.ancestry.com and 1880United States Census, Dauphin Co, PA, FHL 1255123, Film T9-1123, p 298C, www.familysearch.org.

47   Wittle household, 1930 United States Census, Dauphin Co, PA, Roll T626 2026, p 5A, ED54, Image 0725, ancestry.com & Microfilm, PA State Library, Hbg, PA.

48   Minich household, 1880 United States Census, Lancaster Co, PA, ancestry.com & Microfilm, PA State Library, Hbg, PA.

49   Mary Wiittle, Directory 1893, Harrisburg, Dauphin Co, PA.

50   Johney Stewart, Orphans Court, Cumberland County, PA, 1898.

51   John Martin Louis Stewart, 1936, PA, SS-5, Treasury Department, IRS.

52   John Martin Louis Stewart, WW I Draft Reg Cards, 1917-1918 Record, www.ancestry.com.

53   John Stewart, March 1976, PA, Social Security Death Index, www.familysearch.org.

54   Kathleen A Stewart death certificate, #3457571, October 1981, Department of Vital Records, New Castle, PA.

55   Kathleen (Anna) Shover Stewart, 1937, SS-5, Treasury Department, IRS.

56   Kathleen Stewart, August 1902, PA, Social Security Death Index, www.familysearch.org.

57   Stewart household, 1900 United States Census, Cumberland Co, PA, ancestry.com &Microfilm, PA State Library, Hbg, PA.

58   Stewart household, 1900 United States Census, Dauphin Co, PA, T1274, Roll 688, ED 0014,visit 0425, ancestry.com & Microfilm, PA State Library, Hbg, PA.

59   Stewart household, 1910 United States Census, Dauphin Co, PA, T1274, Roll 688, ED 0014,visit 0425, ancestry.com & Microfilm, PA State Library, Hbg, PA.

60   John Stewart, 1930 Harrisburg City Directory, Judith Bennett,jabennett747@adelphia.net.

61   John Stewart, 1930 Harrisburg City Directory, www.ancestry.com.

62   Jacob F Stewart, Death Certificate, #3921009, File #31227, Reg #117, 1950, Dept of Vital Records, New Castle, PA.

63   Kathleen A. Stewart (Thomas), East Harrisburg Cemetery Co, Harrisburg, PA, Section 42, Lot 56, Blk.A.

64   Smith household, 1910 United States Census, Dauphin Co, PA, ancestry.com & Microfilm, PA State Library, Hbg, PA.

65   Smith household, 1910 United States Census, Dauphin Co, PA, T1274, Roll 688, ED 0068,Visit 0046, ancestry.com & Microfilm, PA State Library, Hbg, PA.

66   Kathleen S Stewart, Social Security numident record, application for SS-5, SSA, Nov 2006,Baltimore, MD.

67   Kathleen (Anna) Shover Stewart, 1937, SS-5, Treasury Department, IRS.

68   Kathleen Stewart, October 1981, PA, Social Security Death Index, www.familysearch.org.

69   Frank Acri, US Naturalization Records, Original Documents, 1795-1972, Middle Dt of PA, Petitions #1-500, M1626, Oct 1902.

70   Frank Acri, US Passport Applications, 1795-1925, Oct 1913, Steelton, PA, M1490.

71   Frank Acri, Probate files, 1911, Bk M, Vol 2, p 494-5, Dauphin County Courthouse, Reg of Wills, Deborah Hershey, Elizabethtown, PA, Mar 2008.

72   Frank Acri death certificate, #0795055, File # 23502, Registered #253, PA Vital records, New Castle, PA.

73   Acri-Curcio marriage record, Allegheny County, PA, 1891, #1619, series B.

74   Teresa Acri death certificate, #1172148, File # 84824, Registered #1522, PA Vital records, New Castle, PA.

75   Acri-Curcio marriage record, July 22, 1875, Clerk of Orphans Court, Allegheny Co, PA, 1891.

76   Teresa Acri, Probate files, 1951, #796-1951, Dauphin County Courthouse, Reg of Wills, Deborah Hershey, Elizabethtown, PA, Mar 2008.

77   Franjensco Acri, Catholic Cemeteries, Harrisburg, PA, Block L, Lot 139A-140A.

78   Vencia household, 1900 United States Census, Western PA Genealogical Society and 1900United States Census, Series T623, Film 1403, bk 2, p 47, www.ancestry.com, Judith Kaufman.

79   Franjensco Acri, Ellis Island Passenger Arrivals, 1892-1924, AFI History center,www.ellisisland.org.

80   Francesco Acri, List or Manifest of Alien Immigrants for the ?, NY Passenger Lists,1820-1957, New York, NY, www.ancestry.com.

81   Francesco Acri, Ellis Island Passenger Arrivals, 1892-1924, AFI History center,www.ellisisland.org.

82   Francesco Acri, August 8, 1899, Aller, Ellis Island Passenger Arrivals: AFIHC, manifest 0028, www.ellisisland.org.

83   Acri-Curcio marriage record, Clerk of Orphans Court, Allegheny Co, PA, 1891.

84   Acri family information, St. Mary's Church, Sharpsburg, Allegheny Co, PA in 1892, Dennis Malto,matlod@mindspring.com.

85   Teresa Acri, Catholic Cemeteries, Harrisburg, PA, Block L, Lot 139A, Space 2nd.

86   Vencia household, 1930 United States Census, Allegheny Co, PA, ancestry.com & Microfilm, PA State Library, Hbg, PA.

87   Teresa Curcio, 1893, Charles Martel, Ellis Island Passenger Arrivals: AFIHC, manifest0713, www.ellisisland.org.

88   Teresa Curcio, Ellis Island Passenger Arrivals, 1892-1924, AFI History center,www.ellisisland.org.

89   Teresa Curcio, List or Manifest of Alien Immigrants ?, NY Passenger Lists, 1820-1957,New York, NY, www.ancestry.com.

90   Teresa Acri, US City Directories, Hbg, PA 1875-1946, www.ancestry.com.

91   Teresa Acri, 1930, Harrisburg City Directory, www.distantcousin.com.

92   Teresa Curchi Acri, Death record, Patricia Weidemen, 2006, Weideman Funeral Home, Steelton, PA.

93   Michael Acri, Registration card, Serial #24, Reg #63, WWI Reg Cards,www.ancestry.com.

94   Raymond F Barbush death certificate, #0795113, Reg # 1284, PA Vital records, New Castle, PA.

95   Raimondo Barbuscio, January 25, 1880, FHL, Individual record, CD 43, Pin 258981, www.familysearch.org.

96   Raimondo Barbuscio, FHL, Individual record, CD 43, Pin 258981, www.familysearch.org.

97   Maria Assunta De Stefano, Certifcato di Morte, 1918, Ufficio di Stato Civile, Comune di Castiglione Cosentino, Prov. di Cosenza, Antonio Russo, 2006.

98   Raymond F. Barbush, Catholic Cemeteries, Harrisburg, PA, Section D, Lot 23-25, Space 4-D25.

99   Barbusha household, 1900 United States Census, Luzerne Co, PA, ancestry.com & Microfilm, PA State Library, Hbg, PA.

100   Barbush household, 1910 United States Census, Luzerne Co, PA, ancestry.com & Microfilm, PA State Library, Hbg, PA.

101   Raimondo Barbuscio, Ellis Island Passenger Arrivals, 1892-1924, AFI History center,www.ellisisland.org.

102   Raymond Rosario Barbush, U.S. World War II Draft Registration Cards, 1942, www.ancestry.com.

103   Raymond Barbush, New York Passenger Lists, List of United States Citizens, www.ancestry.com.

104   Raymond (Annie) Barbush, 1930, Harrisburg PA, Directory, www.ancestry.com.

105   Raimondo Barbuscio, Birth Certificate, Ministero per i Beni e le Attivita Culturali,Archivio di Stato di Cosenza, Via Miceli, Cosenza.

106   Bowerman family, Ancestry World Tree project, awt.ancestry.com, David Bowerman,bowerman@kua.net.

107   Jacob H Wittle, Headstones provided for deceased Union Civil War Veterans, 1879-1903, PA, Mar 1879, scanned image, www.ancestry.com.

108   Catherine Whittle death certificate, #0795053, File #107503, Reg # 1052, November 1907, PA Vitals Records, New Castle, PA.

109   Catherine (Mary Kate) Wittle, East Harrisburg Cemetery Listing, #59, 7/23/2005, Karl Fox, CAGS.

110   Jacob H Wittle, Headstones provided for deceased Union Civil War Veterans, 1879-1903, PA, Mar 1879, scanned image, www.ancestry.com.

111   Weidle household, 1840 United States Census, Lancaster Co, PA, ancestry.com & Microfilm, PA State Library, Hbg, PA.

112   Wittle (Witble) household, 1850 United States Census, Lancaster Co, PA, ancestry.com & Microfilm, PA State Library, Hbg, PA.

113   Wittel household, 1860 United States Census, Dauphin Co, PA, ancestry.com & Microfilm, PA State Library, Hbg, PA.

114   Jacob Wittle, Civil War Pension Index, 201, PA Infantry, filed 188?, www.ancestry.com.

115   500 Years of Wittels and Related Families, William T. Wittel, June 2000, Marietta, GA.

116   Catherine Wittle, East Harrisburg Cemetery Co, Harrisburg, PA, Section 19, Lot 74.

117   Kile household, 1840 United States Census, Lancaster Co, PA, ancestry.com & Microfilm, PA State Library, Hbg, PA.

118   Brubaker household, 1850 United States Census, Lancaster Co, PA, ancestry.com & Microfilm, PA State Library, Hbg, PA.

119   Wittle household, 1880 United States Census, Lancaster Co, PA, Roll T9-1141, p 203A, ED131, Image 0411, ancestry.com & Microfilm, PA State Library, Hbg, PA.

120   Wenrick household, 1900 United States Census, Dauphin Co, PA, ancestry.com & Microfilm, PA State Library, Hbg, PA.

121   Kate Wittle, US City Directories, Hbg, PA 1875-1946, www.ancestry.com.

122   Roddy records, Genevieve Roddy, PA.

123   Henry Minnick death record, #3571367, File # 12004, Reg # 219, 1907, Dauphin Co, PA, Department of Vital records, New Castle, PA.

124   Minnick household, 1900 United States Census, Dauphin Co, PA, ancestry.com & Microfilm, PA State Library, Hbg, PA.

125   Lucy A Minnick death certificate, #88754, #3328061, September 1924, Department of Vital Records, New Castle, PA.

126   J Henry Minick, Index card burial record, Sec T, Lot 45, Space 1, Harrisburg Cemetery Ass'n, Harrisburg, PA.

127   Hergershimer household, 1860 United States Federal Census, Philadelphia, PA, ancestry.com &Microfilm, PA State Library, Hbg, PA.

128   Minich household, 1870 United States Census, Dauphin Co, PA, Roll M593-1334, p 290,Image 593, Georgette Ochs, tetlin@hotmail.com.

129   Minich household, 1870 United States Census, Dauphin Co, PA, ancestry.com & Microfilm, PA State Library, Hbg, PA.

130   Minich household, 1860 United States Census, Lancaster Co, PA, ancestry.com & Microfilm, PA State Library, Hbg, PA.

131   Henry Minnick, Civil War Veterans Card File, 1861-1866, PA State Archives,www.digitalarchives.state.pa.us.

132   Henry Minnick, Civil War Pension Index: General Index to Pension Files, 1861-1934, www.ancestry.com.

133   Henry Minnick death record, Civil War Pension Index, F 127 and G 55, PA Infantry, filed 1896,1907, www.ancestry.com.

134   Henry Minick, American Civil War Records, HDS, 1999-, www.ancestry.com.

135   Henry Minich, Civil War Veterans Card File, 1861-1866, PA State Archives,www.digitalarchives.state.pa.us.

136   John Henry Minick, Probate files, 1907, Bk R, p50, file 18, microfilm roll 34, Dauphin County Courthouse, Reg of Wills, Deborah Hershey, Elizabethtown, PA, Mar 2008.

137   J Henry Minick, Index card burial record, Sec T, Lot 45, Space 2, Harrisburg Cemetery Ass'n, Harrisburg, PA.

138   Sheets household, 1850 United States Census, Dauphin Co, PA, Pam Patton, poohie@penn.com.

139   Sheets household, 1850 United States Census, Dauphin Co, PA, p 328, Roll M432-775,ancestry.com & Microfilm, PA State Library, Hbg, PA.

140   Seibtone household, 1860 United States Census, Dauphin Co, PA, ancestry.com & Microfilm, PA State Library, Hbg, PA.

141   Minnick household, 1900 United States Census, Dauphin Co, PA, ancestry.com & Microfilm, PA State Library, Hbg, PA.

142   Minnick household, 1910 United States Census, Dauphin Co, PA, T1274, Roll 688, ED 0068,visit 0074, ancestry.com & Microfilm, PA State Library, Hbg, PA.

143   Minich household, 1920 United States Census, Dauphin Co, PA, Roll T625 1558, p 3A, ED75, Image 0136, ancestry.com & Microfilm, PA State Library, Hbg, PA.

144   Sheets household, 1850 United States Census, Dauphin Co, PA, Pam Patton,poohie@penn.com.

145   Seibtone household, 1860 United States Census, Dauphin Co, PA, ancestry.com & Microfilm PA State Library, Hbg, PA.

146   Minnich household, 1920 United States Census, Dauphin Co, PA, Roll T625 1558, p 3A, ED75, Image 0136, ancestry.com & Microfilm, PA State Library, Hbg, PA.

147   Jacob Stewart, FHL, Individual Record, www.familysearch.org.

148   Matilda Stewart death record, #3520761, #79566, Reg # 876, September 1938, Department of Vitral Records, New Castle, PA.

149   Stewart household, 1870 United States Census, Cumberland Co, PA, ancestry.com &Microfilm, PA State Library, Hbg, PA.

150   Stewart household, 1880 United States Census, Cumberland Co, PA, FHL 1255121, FilmT9-1121, p 31A, www.familysearch.com.

151   Spong-Stewart, Application for Marriage License, No 250-25, Commonwealth of PA, County of Cumberland.

152   McKinsey household, 1880 United States Census, Cumberland Co, PA, FHL 1255121, FilmT9-1121, p 20D, www.familysearch.com.

153   Stwert (sic) household, 1930 United States Census, Cumberland Co, PA, Roll T626 2025, p 14A,ED 54, Image 0899, ancestry.com & Microfilm, PA State Library, Hbg, PA.

154   Robert Charles Shover, WW I Draft Reg Cards, 1917-1918 Record, www.ancestry.com.

155   Robert C Shover, death certificate, #3571259, File #45367, Reg #567, May 1933,Department of Vital Records, New Castle, PA.

156   Shover-Shannon Marriage record, Cumberland County, PA, January 1899, #V-1-318.

157   Bessie Heinbaugh, Pennsylvania, Death Certificates, 1906-1944 about Mrs Bessie Heinbaugh, ancestry.com.

158   Robert C Shover, Burial #85, 106, C, Grave 1, May 8, 1933, Rolling Green Cemetery, Camp Hill, PA c/o Sherry Blumanstock.

159   Shover household, 1880 United States Census, Cumberland Co, PA, www.ancestry.com and1880 United States Census, Cumberland Co, PA, FHL 1255122, Film T9-1122, p 484C, www.familysearch.com.

160   Shover household, 1900 United States Federal Census about Charles L Shover, ancestry.com.

161   Kimberline household, 1920 United States Census, Cumberland Co, PA, ancestry.com &Microfilm, PA State Library, Hbg, PA.

162   Shover household, 1930 United States Census, Dauphin Co, PA, Roll T626 2027, p 9A, ED65, Image 0504, ancestry.com & Microfilm, PA State Library, Hbg, PA.

163   Shover household, 1930 United States Census, Judith Bennett, jabennett747@adelphia.net.

164   Shover household, 1930 Harrisburg City Directory, Judith Bennett,jabennett747@adelphia.net.

165   Michael Curcio, Consent to the Marriage of a Child or Ward, Clerk of Orphans Court, Allegheny Co, PA, 1891.

166   Pasquale Barbuscio, FHL, Individual record, CD 43, Pin 256975, www.familysearch.org.

167   Buela/Buglio Family, Cassandra Buela, cassybuela@yahoo.com, ancestry world tree project, www.ancestry.com.

168   Carmina "Catarina" Buglio, FHL, Individual record, CD 43, Pin 257134, www.familysearch.org.

169   Pasquale Barbuscio, Ellis Island Passenger Arrivals, 1892-1924, AFI History center,www.ellisisland.org.

170   Wittel household, 1820 United States Census, Lancaster Co, PA, ancestry.com & Microfilm, PA State Library, Hbg, PA.

171   Wittel household, 1830 United States Census, Lancaster Co, PA, Roll M19 153, p 367,Image 720, ancestry.com & Microfilm, PA State Library, Hbg, PA.

172   Widdel household, 1850 United States Census, Lancaster Co, PA, Roll M432-787, p 354,Image 707, ancestry.com & Microfilm, PA State Library, Hbg, PA.

173   Wittle (Witble) household, 1860 United States Census, Lancaster Co, PA, ancestry.com & Microfilm, PA State Library, Hbg, PA.

174   John Wittle, Estate Inventory 1869, b132, f15, Marge Bardeen, 2006, Lancaster County Historical Society, Lancaster, PA.

175   Hummer family information, Zion Church, Manheim, Lancaster Co, PA, 1771-, Lancaster County Historical Society.

176   Wittle (Witble) household, 1870 United States Census, Lancaster Co, PA, ancestry.com & Microfilm PA State Library, Hbg, PA.

177   Kyle household, 1830 United States Census, Lancaster Co, PA, ancestry.com & Microfilm,PA State Library, Hbg, PA.

178   Elizabeth Minnich, Death record, Lancaster Co Record Mgmt, March 1904, Lancaster Co, PA.

179   Mining household, 1840 United States Census, Dauphin, PA, ancestry.com & Microfilm, PA State Library, Hbg, PA.

180   Minich household, 1850 United States Census, Lancaster Co, PA, ancestry.com & Microfilm, PA State Library, Hbg, PA.

181   Minich household, 1860 United States Census, Lancaster Co, PA, ancestry.com & Microfilm, PA State Library, Hbg, PA.

182   Minnich household, 1870 United States Census, Lancaster Co, PA, ancestry.com & Microfilm, PA State Library, Hbg, PA.

183   Sheetz family information, Rob Sheetz, Robsheetz32@wmconnect.com.

184   George Sheetz, Probate files, 1884, rep 50, Perry County Historians, Newport, PA, Deborah Hershey, Elizabethtown, PA, Jan 2009.

185   George Sheets, Bob Sheetz, Robsheetz32@wmconnect.com.

186   George Sheets, William McKim affidavit, Perry Historians, Newport, PA.

187   Mary McKim Sheets, St. Paul/Bauerman Lutheran & Reformed, Enterline, PA, The Perry Historians.

188   Sheetz household, 1820 United States Census, Dauphin Co, PA, ancestry.com & Microfilm, PA State Library, Hbg, PA.

189   Sheetz household, 1840 United States Census, Dauphin Co, PA ancestry.com & Microfilm, PA State Library, Hbg, PA.

190   Sheetz household, 1860 United States Census, Perry Co, PA, The Perry Historians.

191   Sheets household, 1870 United States Census, Perry Co, PA, The Perry Historians.

192   Sheets household, 1880 United States Census, Perry Co, PA, ancestry.com & Microfilm, PA State Library, Hbg, PA.

193   Sheets household, 1860 United States Census, Perry Co, PA, The Perry Historians.

194   McKim household, 1820 United States Census, Cumberland Co, PA, ancestry.com &Microfilm, PA State Library, Hbg, PA.

195   McKim household, 1830 United States Census, Cumberland Co, PA, ancestry.com &Microfilm, PA State Library, Hbg, PA.

196   Sheets household, 1860 United States Census, Dauphin Co, PA, ancestry.com & Microfilm, PA State Library, Hbg, PA.

197   Sheetz household, 1870 United States Census, Dauphin Co, PA, ancestry.com & Microfilm, PA State Library, Hbg, PA.

198   Sheets household, 1880 United States Census, Dauphin, A, ancestry.com & Microfilm, PA State Library, Hbg, PA.

199   Sheetz household, 1870 United States Census, Dauphin Co, PA, ancestry.com & Microfilm, PA State Library, Hbg, PA.

200   George Sheets, Probate files, 1884, rep 50, Perry County Historians, Newport, PA, Deborah Hershey, Elizabethtown, PA, Jan 2009.

201   Elizabeth Scheetz, St. Paul/Bauerman Lutheran & Reformed Church, Enterline, PA, The Perry Historians.

202   Louis L Stewart burial record, 1876, Brick Church, near West Fairview, Cumberland County, CumberlandCounty Historical Society.

203   Louis L Stewart, Brick Church, Cumberland County, Tammy Putt, Enola, PA, Lot 1-269.

204   Louis L Stewart, Cumberland County PA Cemetery & Necrology Records, PA State Library, Harrisburg, PA, J. Zeamer, H.I. Harman, p 169, Janet Wright, j.wright@comcast.net.

205   Martha E Stewart death certificate, Cover letter, Cumberland County Historical Society.

206   Martha E Stewart death certificate, Zion (Brick) Lutheran, Enola, Cumberland Co, PA, p 27, Janet Wrightj.wright@comcast.net.

207   Martha E Stewart death certificate, #3179505, File #11887, January 1926, PA Vitals Records, New Castle, PA.

208   Martha Etta Stewart, Brick Church, Cumberland County, Tammy Putt, Enola, PA, Lot 1-269.

209   Martha E Stewart, Probate files, 1925, Bk 33, p296, #1098, Cumberland County Courthouse, Reg of Wills, Deborah Hershey, Elizabethtown, PA, Mar 2008.

210   Martha E Stewart death certificate, #11887, #3457534, January 1926, Department of Vital Records, New Castle, PA.

211   Lewis L Stewart, Judith Bennett, jabennett747@adelphia.net.

212   Stewart household, 1840 United States Census, Dauphin Co, PA, ancestry.com & Microfilm, PA State Library, Hbg, PA.

213   Stewart household, 1850 United States Census, Dauphin Co, PA, ancestry.com & Microfilm, PA State Library, Hbg, PA.

214   Stewart family information, Joe Stewart c/o Judith Bennett, jabennett747@adelphia.net.

215   Martha Etta Stewart, Stewart information, Judy Bennett, jabennett747@adelphia.net.

216   Haldeman household, 1860 United States Census, Lancaster Co, PA, ancestry.com.

217   Guyer household, 1910 United States Census, Cumberland Co, PA, ED 0013, Visit 0009,ancestry.com & Microfilm, PA State Library, Hbg, PA.

218   Stewart household, 1920 United States Census, Cumberland Co, PA, ancestry.com &Microfilm, PA State Library, Hbg, PA.

219   Guyer household, 1910 United States Census, Cumberland Co, PA, ED 0013, Visit 0009,ancestry.com & Microfilm, PA State Library, Hbg, PA.

220   Guyer household, Guyer household, 1910 United States Census, Cumberland Co, PA, ED0013, Visit 0009, www.ancestry.com.

221   McKinsey-Frey, Marriage record, York County Historical Society, c/o Jerianne Barnes,jlbarnes@wnynet.net.

222   Susan McKinsy, #94154, #3457521, October 1909, Department of Vital Records, New Castle, PA.

223   Susan McKinsey, Brick Church, Cumberland County, Tammy Putt, Enola, PA, Lot 2-047.

224   James McKinsey, Zion (Brick) Lutheran, Enola, Cumberland Co, PA,p 9, Janet Wrightj.wright@comcast.net.

225   McKinstry household, 1840 United States Census, Cumberland Co, PA ancestry.com & Microfilm, PA State Library, Hbg, PA.

226   McKinsey household, 1850 United States Census, York Co, PA, Roll M432 840, p223, ancestry.com & Microfilm, PA State Library, Hbg, PA.

227   McKinsey household, 1860 United States Census, York Co, PA, Roll M653 1201, p472, ancestry.com & Microfilm, PA State Library, Hbg, PA.

228   McKinsey household, 1870 United States Census, Cumberland Co, PA, ancestry.com &Microfilm, PA State Library, Hbg, PA.

229   McKinsey household, 1880 United States Census, Cumberland Co, PA, www.ancestry.com and1880 United States Census, Cumberland Co, PA, FHL 1255121, Film T9-1121, p 20D, www.familysearch.com.

230   McKinsey household, 1860 United States Census, York Co, PA, Roll M653 1201, p472 ,ancestry.com & Microfilm, PA State Library, Hbg, PA.

231   McKinsey household, McKinsey household, 1850 United States Census, York Co, PA, Roll M432840, p 223, ancestry.com & Microfilm, PA State Library, Hbg, PA.

232   McKinsey household, 1870 United States Census, Cumberland Co, PA, ancestry.com &Microfilm, PA State Library, Hbg, PA.

233   Matilda Stewart death record, #3520761, #79566, Reg # 876, September 1938, Department of Vital Records, New Castle, PA.

234   Susan McKinsey, Zion (Brick) Lutheran, Enola, Cumberland Co, PA, p 9, Janet Wrightj.wright@comcast.net.

235   Frey household, 1850 United States Federal Census, York Co, PA ancestry.com &Microfilm, PA State Library, Hbg, PA.

236   McKinsey household, 1860 United States Census, York Co, PA, ancestry.com & Microfilm, PA State Library, Hbg, PA.

237   McKinsey household, 1880 United States Census, Cumberland Co, PA, www.ancestry.com and1880 United States Census, Cumberland Co, PA, FHL 1255121, Film T9-1121, p 20D, www.familysearch.com.

238   Mrs.. James McKinsey, October 1909, Carlisle Evening Sentinel obituary, Janet Wrightj.wright@comcast.net.

239   John B Shover death certificate, #3586793, File #28883, Reg #370, Dauphin Co, PA, 1917, Department of Vital Records, New castle, PA.

240   Margaret Shover death certificate, Dauphin County Register of Wills, bk G, #718, December 17, 1903, Harrisburg, PA.

241   Margaret T Shover, East Harrisburg Cemetery Listing, #59, 7/23/2005, Karl Fox, CAGS.

242   Shover household, 1900 United States Census, Dauphin Co, PA, ancestry.com & Microfilm, PA State Library, Hbg, PA.

243   John E Shover, East Harrisburg Cemetery Listing, #59, 7/23/2005, Karl Fox, CAGS.

244   Shover household, 1860 United States Census, Cumberland Co, PA, ancestry.com &Microfilm, PA State Library, Hbg, PA.

245   Shover household, 1870 United States Census, Cumberland Co, PA, ancestry.com &Microfilm, PA State Library, Hbg, PA.

246   Shover household, 1900 United States Census, Dauphin Co, PA, ancestry.com & Microfilm, PA State Library, Hbg, PA.

247   John Shover, Civil War Pension Index: General Index to Pension Files, 1861-1934, www.ancestry.com.

248   John Shover, Civil War Soldiers & Sailors System, www.itd.nps.gov/cwss.

249   John Shover, Civil War Pension app, App #1227691, Cert #988143 & App #788558 Cert#559453, fotenote.com.

250   Shover household, 1880 United States Census, Cumberland Co, PA, ancestry.com &Microfilm, PA State Library, Hbg, PA.

251   Piper household, 1860 United States Census, Franklin Co, PA, ancestry.com & Microfilm, PA State Library, Hbg, PA.

252   Piper household, 1870 United States Census, Dauphin Co, PA, ancestry.com & Microfilm, PA State Library, Hbg, PA.

253   Shover household, 1880 United States Census, Dauphin Co, PA, ancestry.com & Microfilm, PA State Library, Hbg, PA.

254   Shannon-Reath, Application for Marriage License, Commonwealth of PA, County of Cumberland, Index bk 23, 133, 1915, c/o Cumberland County Register of Wills, Carlisle, PA.

255   Cyrus Shannon death certificate, #843, May 1901, Cumberland County Register of Wills, Carlisle, PA.

256   Shanon household, 1900 United States Census, Cumberland Co, PA, Series T623 1401, bk 1,p 206, ancestry.com & Microfilm, PA State Library, Hbg, PA.

257   Shannon household, 1900 US federal census, Cumberland, PA, www.ancestry.com.

258   Cyrus Shannon, Probate files, 1901, Bk W, p285, #645, Cumberland County Courthouse, Reg of Wills, Deborah Hershey, Elizabethtown, PA, Mar 2008.

259   Cyrus Shannon death certificate, #843, May 1901, Cumberland County Register of Wills, Carlisle, PA.

260   Ceynis Shannon, Records In Stone II, Edward L. Shaeffer, 1982, Shippensburg Historical Society, Cumberland Country Historical Society.

261   Shanon household, 1860 United States Census, Cumberland Co, PA, Series M653, Roll 1102,Part 1, p 695, ancestry.com & Microfilm, PA State Library, Hbg, PA.

262   Shanon household, 1870 United States Census, Cumberland Co, PA, Series M593, Roll 1333,Part 1, p 473A, ancestry.com & Microfilm, PA State Library, Hbg, PA.

263   Shanon household, 1880 United States Census, ED 88, p 455, ancestry.com & Microfilm, PA State Library, Hbg, PA, Janet Stacey.

264   Cyrus J Shannon, American Civil War Soldiers Records, HDS, 1999-, ancestry.com &Microfilm, PA State Library, Hbg, PA.

265   Cyrus J Shannon, 1890 Veterans Schedule, private, Southampton, Cumberland Co, PA, Roll86, p 3, ED 119, www.ancestry.com.

266   Cyrus J Shannon, [Cyrus J Shannon, Civil War Pension App, App#840411, Cert # 677423,fotenote.com.

267   Shannon household, 1880 United States Census, ED 88, p 455, www.ancestry.com, Janet Stacey and 1880 United States Census, www.familysearch.org.

268   Cyrus Shannon, March 1901, Last Will and Testament, Cumberland Co, PA, #285, Cumberland County Historical Society.

269   Cyrus W Shannon, 1864-5 service, 1890 Veterans Schedule, private, Southampton, Cumberland Co, PA, Roll 86, p 3, ED 119, www.ancestry.com.

270   Shannon household, Application for Marriage License, Commonwealth of PA, County of Cumberland, Index bk 23, 133, 1915, c/o Cumberland County Register of Wills, Carlisle, PA.

271   Mary Shannon death certificate, #841, May 1901, Cumberland County Register of Wills, Carlisle, PA.

272   Mary C Shannon, Records In Stone II, Edward L. Shaeffer, 1982, Shippensburg Historical Society, Cumberland Country Historical Society.

273   Shanon household, 1880 United States Census, ED 88, p 455, www.anccstry.com, Janet Stacey and 1880 United States Census, www.familysearch.org.

274   Shannon household, 1900 United States Census, Cumberland Co, PA, Series T623 1401, bk 1,p 206, ancestry.com & Microfilm, PA State Library, Hbg, PA.

275   Gaetano Barbuscio, FHL, Individual record, CD 43, Pin 256273, www.familysearch.org.

276   Orsala Marsico, FHL, Individual record, CD 43, Pin 256274, www.familysearch.org.

277   Carmine Mario "Francesco" Buglio, FHL, Individual record, CD 43, Pin 255270, www.familysearch.org.

278   Giuseppina Magnelli, FHL, Individual record, CD 43, Pin 255804, www.familysearch.org.

279   Maria Acri, Certifcato di Morte, 1910, Ufficio di Stato Civile, Comune di Castiglione Cosentino, Prov. di Cosenza, Antonio Russo, 2006.

280   Jacob Wittel, Penryn Union Cemetery (Penn Twp.), Manheim Historical Society, Manheim, PA.

281   500 Years of Wittels and Related Families, William T. Wittel, June 2000, Marietta, GA.

282   Johann Jacob Wittel, Ancestors of Johann Jacob Wittel, www.familybranches.org/32.htm.

283   Wittle (Witble) household, 1820 United States Census, Lancaster Co, PA, ancestry.com & Microfilm, PA State Library, Hbg, PA.

284   Wittel household, 1830 United States Census, Lancaster Co, PA, ancestry.com & Microfilm, PA State Library, Hbg, PA.

285   Wittle (Witble) household, 1840 United States Census, Lancaster Co, PA, ancestry.com & Microfilm, PA State Library, Hbg, PA.

286   Jacob Wittel, October 1805, Fair American, Passenger Arrivals at the Port of Philadelphia, 1800-1819, p 782, www.myfamily.com.

287   Jacob Wittel, PA Census, 1772-1890, Philadelphia, PA, www.ancestry.com.

288   Anna Wittel, Penryn Union Cemetery (Penn Twp.), Manheim Historical Society, Manheim, PA.

289   George Sheets Jr, FHL, Individual record, www.familysearch.org.

290   Maria Sheetz, St. Paul/Bauerman Lutheran & Reformed Church, Enterline, PA, The Perry Historians.

291   Shetz household, 1800 United States Census, Dauphin Co, PA, ancestry.com & Microfilm, PA State Library, Hbg, PA.

292   Sheetz household, 1810 United States Census, Dauphin Co, PA, Series M252, Roll 54, Part1, p 99, ancestry.com & Microfilm, PA State Library, Hbg, PA.

293   Shetz household, 1820 United States Census, Dauphin Co, PA, ancestry.com & Microfilm, PA State Library, Hbg, PA.

294   Schitz family information, PA Births, Dauphin County, J. Humphrey.

295   William Sheets, St. Paul/Bauerman Lutheran & Reformed Church, Enterline, PA, The Perry Historians.

296   Valentine Family Tree, Garry Valentine, 2002, ivalentine2@msn.com,\http://wc.rootsweb.com/cgi-bin/igm.cgi?op=AHN&db=:2235272&id=I12 1297012.

297   James McKim, Probate files, 1835, pA284, A369, Cumberland County Courthouse, Reg of Wills, Deborah Hershey, Elizabethtown, PA, Mar 20.

298   McKim household, 1810 United States Census, Cumberland Co, PA, ancestry.com &Microfilm, PA State Library, Hbg, PA.

299   James McKim, Probate files, 1831, Letter of Admin, D105, Inv #522, Cumberland County Courthouse, Reg of Wills, Deborah Hershey, Elizabethtown, PA, Mar 2008.

300   James McKim, Probate files, 1835, pA284, A369, Cumberland County Courthouse, Reg of Wills, Deborah Hershey, Elizabethtown, PA, Mar 2008.

301   Stewart household, 1830 United States Census, Dauphin Co, PA, ancestry.com & Microfilm, PA State Library, Hbg, PA.

302   Stewart household, 1860 United States Census, Dauphin Co, PA, ancestry.com & Microfilm, PA State Library, Hbg, PA.

303   Louer household, 1870 United States Census, Dauphin Co, PA, ancestry.com & Microfilm, PA State Library, Hbg, PA.

304   Smith household, 1830 United States Census, Lancaster Co, PA, ancestry.com & Microfilm, PA State Library, Hbg, PA.

305   Smith household, 1840 United States Census, Lancaster Co, PA, ancestry.com & Microfilm, PA State Library, Hbg, PA.

306   McKinsey household, 1810 United States Census, www.ancstry.com.

307   Henry Fry, York County Records, York County Archives, York Co, PA.

308   Fry household, 1820 United States Census, York Co, PA, ancestry.com.

309   Frey household, 1830 United States Census, York Co, PA, ancestry.com, Series M33, Roll114. p 65, Gail Steckel, gail@gregsteckel.com.

310   Fry household, 1840 United States Census, York Co, PA, ancestry.com.

311   Frey household, 1850 United States Census, York Co, PA, ancestry.com.

312   Frey household, 1850 United States Census, York Co, PA, ancestry.com.

313   Henry Fry, Probate files, 1863, Rep 32, York County Archives, York, PA, Deborah Hershey, Elizabethtown, PA, Dec 2008.

314   Fry household, 1850 United States Census, York Co, PA, ancestry.com.

315   Sebastian Shover death record abstract, 1892, Spring Hill Church, Shippensburg, Cumberland County, PA, Cumberland County Historical Society.

316   Sebastian Shover, Probate files, 1839, Letter of Admin, docket G385, Cumberland County Courthouse, Reg of Wills, Deborah Hershey, Elizabethtown, PA, Mar 2008.

317   Sebastian Shover, Deaths, German Reformed, Shippensburg, PA, Cumberland County Historical Society.

318   Sebastian Shover, Obituary People's Register, June 3, 1892, SHOVER, Sebastian c/o BonitaM. Bingaman, Greencastle, PA.

319   Shober family information, German Reformed, Shippensburg, Cumberland County Historical Society, Carlisle, PA.

320   Anna Eliza Shover, Cover letter, Cumberland County Historical Society.

321   Anna Eliza. Shover, German Reformed, Shippensburg, Register, Cumberland County Historical Society.

322   Sebastian Shover, Spring Hill Cemetery, Shippensburg, Cumberland County Historical Society.

323   Shover household, 1850 United States Census, Cumberland Co, PA, ancestry.com &Microfilm, PA State Library, Hbg, PA.

324   Shaver household, 1870 United States Census, Cumberland Co, PA, ancestry.com &Microfilm, PA State Library, Hbg, PA.

325   Sebastian Shover, Civil War Pension Index, 209, PA infantry, filed 1891, 1892,www.ancestry.com.

326   Sebastian Shover, American Civil War Soldiers Records, HDS, 1999-, www.ancestry.com.

327   Shover research, Shippensburg Township Tax Rates, 1880, 1881, 1882, Cumberland County Historical Society, Carlisle, PA.

328   Shover research, Cumberland County Historical Society, Carlisle, PA.

329   Shover household, 1900 United States Census, Cumberland Co, PA, ancestry.com &Microfilm, PA State Library, Hbg, PA.

330   Piper family information, One tree, from WFT collection, trees.ancestry.com/owt,www.ancestry.com.

331   Adam Piper, 1728-1788, Fannett Township, Franklin Co, PA, pp50-51 c/o Bonita M.Bingaman, Greencastle, PA.

332   George Piper, Stone vol III, Shippensburg Historical Society, Edward L Shaeffer, Scott, RAOGK Volunteer, maizeblue6@comcast.net.

333   Piper household, 1850 United States Census, Franklin Co, PA, ancestry.com & Microfilm, PA State Library, Hbg, PA.

334   Piper household, 1880 United States Census, Cumberland, PA, ancestry.com & Microfilm, PA State Library, IIbg, PA.

335   Piper household, 1870 United States Census, Franklin Co, PA, ancestry.com & Microfilm, PA State Library, Hbg, PA.

336   George Piper, Last Will & Test. of George Piperr, Bk I, Folio 171, Estate #11641,Jan 3, 1881, Franklin Co Courthouse, Chambersburg, PA, Bob Fout, Apr 2008.

337   Agnes Harvey Piper, Stone vol III, Shippensburg Historical Society, Edward L Shaeffer, Scott, RAOGK Volunteer, maizeblue6@comcast.net.

338   Piper   family   information,   One   tree,   from   WFT   collection, trees.ancestry.com/owt,www.ancestry.com, trees.ancestry.com/owt.

339   Shannon household, 1840 United States census, Cumberland Co, PA, ancestry.com & Microfilm, PA State Library, Hbg, PA.

340   Swovler household, 1860 United States Federal Census, Franklin, PA, p288, ancestry.com &Microfilm, PA State Library, Hbg, PA.

341   Swoveland household, 1900 United States Federal Census, Cumberland, PA, SD 9, ED 5, Sheet8, ancestry.com & Microfilm, PA State Library, Hbg, PA.

342   Mrs Peter Schmeltzer, Pennsylvania, Death Certificates, 1906-1944 about Mrs Peter Schmeltzer, ancestry.com.

343   Henry   Swovelan,   Pennsylvania,   Death   Certificates,   1906-1944   for   Henry Swoveland,ancestry.com.

344   Rachael   Swoveland,   Pennsylvania,   Death   Certificates,   1906-1944   about   Rachael Swoveland,ancestry.com.

345   Swoveland household, 1870 United States Federal Census, Cumberland, PA, p344, ancestry.com& Microfilm, PA State Library, Hbg, PA.

346   Swoveland household, 1880 United States Federal Census, Cumberland, PA, p10, ancestry.com &Microfilm, PA State Library, Hbg, PA.

347   Swoveland household, 1910 United States Federal Census, Cumberland, PA, SD 14, ED 9, Sheet9B, ancestry.com & Microfilm, PA State Library, Hbg, PA.